Sea Monsters

SEA MONSTERS

A COLLECTION OF EYEWITNESS ACCOUNTS

James B. Sweeney

DAVID McKAY COMPANY, INC.   NEW YORK

Library of Congress Cataloging in Publication Data

Sweeney, James B
    Sea monsters.

    SUMMARY: A collection of eyewitness reports of sea
monsters which have been sighted as long ago as 700 B.C.
and as recently as 1976.
    1. Sea monsters—Juvenile literature. [1. Sea
monsters] I. Title.
QL89.2.S4S88   001.9'44   77-6105
ISBN 0-679-20424-5

10 9 8 7 6 5 4 3 2 1

Manufactured in the United States of America

Book design by H. Roberts

This book is dedicated to my wife,
the former Lieutenant Helen Ver, U.S.N.

Contents

Introduction

EVER since man first got a look at the sea there have been sea monsters—if not in fact, at least in the imagination of the onlooker. For what lay beneath the surface of the ocean was a mystery.

Life was there, man could be certain of that. Fish were seen jumping and crabs scuttling back into the waves, while sea shells littered the beaches.

And man soon discovered that what did exist in the depths could bite, cut, sting, crush, and pierce. He also noticed that some of the animals causing such damage were big. How big, and how dangerous, no one could say for sure.

So fantasy took over. Lobsters were said to grow so large they could devour men. Whales reportedly reached a length of 1,000 feet and were so broad they were mistaken for islands. It was also rumored that sea bishops, part man and part fish, lived in the depths. The sea was thought to harbor beautiful mermaids, vicious mermen, and powerful gods. It was said that Poseidon, later to be known as Neptune, lived in an ivory castle on the floor of the ocean. Occasionally he surfaced to ride a jeweled chariot, drawn through the clouds by three golden horses.

Many of these things were purely imaginary, but not all. For there were sailors hobbling about as the result of having had a leg snapped off by some big-toothed monster. Now and then a dead ten-armed creature would be washed ashore. Fishing boats had holes stove through their thick planking by beasts that possessed a sword for a snout.

Fact and fancy were intermixed. For centuries stories grew more vivid, more wild, more fascinating. Yet as time went on and men commenced to dive beneath the surface of the ocean, it was found that there really were monstrous animals living in the sea. As a result of this half-true information, sailors tried to relate what they had seen to things known to exist on land. Thus we have the sea lion, the sea elephant, the sea horse, the sea cow, and many other marine animals with land-associated names.

Then came the time for science to emerge. The early Greeks, long before the coming of Christ, began to seek out true facts. Great minds, like Hippocrates, Aristotle, and Archimedes, started to use reasoning in place of fear. They classified some animals of the sea, but there were others they could not group. Some were too elusive and some were too strange.

Centuries later the Romans added to this basic information. With the progression of time, we find explorers, such as Christopher Columbus and Ferdinand Magellan, navigating with the help of maps drafted by artists like Leonardo da Vinci. Charts were drawn of the sea, and out of respect for the unknown, beasts were depicted in open spaces.

In 1823 Charles Darwin, at twenty-three years of age, made his historic voyage around the world as a naturalist. He sailed aboard H.M.S. *Beagle* on an exploratory trip that lasted five years. During this time he recorded a great deal of information about the sea, which helped dispel numerous myths. It also added to the mystery of the sea, for there remained much that seemed inexplicable.

Enlightenment came faster after that. The early 1900s saw the submarine perfected, and what lay beneath the surface of the sea was then given closer attention. As one year followed another, men sounded its depths with electronic gear and attempted to discover all things that lived within its protective darkness. In this they failed. Each year new discoveries are being reported.

During these first million years man has been living on earth, he has not succeeded in exploring the floor of the ocean. Perhaps in the next century or two he will be successful. Meantime, as of today, here is all that man knows about sea monsters, including that elusive beast called "The Loch Ness Monster."

1

The Sea Where They Live

THERE are no sea monsters on the moon. We can be certain of that. For man knows more about the moon than he does about the bottom of the sea. In fact, he knows practically nothing about the bottom of the sea—and it is there that sea monsters lurk.

So, if one is to go looking for sea monsters, one should know something about the world in which they live. It seems to be a world without limits. There are gorges far deeper than any on land. There are flat desert-like areas that would make the African Sahara appear the size of a postage stamp. There are mountain ranges higher, and a good deal longer, than any on the surface of the earth. There are areas of rich fertile soil; there are seemingly endless stretches of wasteland, and, most important of all, there are caves. It is probably in these dens that gigantic aquatic animals lurk.

Unfortunately, there is no light down there by which we might see these huge creatures; it is a black world where sunlight has never penetrated. It is the home for billions and billions of sea creatures, both large and small.

SEA MONSTERS

A scientist once figured that if a single cubic mile of ocean water were to be analyzed, it would yield 82,000,000,000,000,000,000,000,000,000,000,000 particles of sea life, or a figure so large that it is not conceivable by man. Also, it was estimated that in this same cube of water there would be $93 million in gold and many tons of salt, iodine, and magnesium and numerous other valuable commodities. The floor of this cubic mile of ocean water might even be strewn with diamonds and other precious gems. Since there are 330 million cubic miles of water in the sea, it then becomes a mathematical problem to figure how much sea life is in the world's oceans. Multiply 82,000,000,000,000,000,000,000,000,000,000,000 by 330,000,000 and you will have the answer.

Let us look into this cold, unfriendly world in which so many strange forms of life exist. To begin with, three-quarters of the earth's surface is covered with water. If the entire world were made smooth as a bowling ball, both above and below the sea, a layer of water 12,000 feet deep would cover our globe. If this were to happen, the Empire State Building, which is 102 stories high, would be covered by almost 11,000 feet of water. The seemingly bottomless part of the ocean, known as the Mindanao Trench, in the Pacific, is almost 8 miles deep. There are 5,280 feet in a mile, which means that if Mt. Everest, the tallest peak on earth at 29,141 feet, were uprooted and dropped into the Mindanao Trench, it would be covered by almost 9,000 feet of water.

During October of 1976, two young Americans succeeded in climbing to the top of Mt. Everest. They were the fifty-third and fifty-fourth persons to accomplish this feat. Yet in all the history of mankind, only two people have ever managed to come within range of the deepest part of the ocean. In 1960 they made the descent in a U.S. Navy bathyscaphe, a submarine-like vessel. The bathyscaphe, named *Trieste*, descended into the Pacific to a depth of 35,800 feet.

No one has succeeded in any attempt to walk on the bottom of the Mindanao Trench. How can we tell what lives there? Only by the use of electronic devices. That and the word of scientists. Can these machines and human beings be wrong? Of course they can. As we shall see in a following chapter, they were in error about at least one fish, the coelacanth. They could be wrong about other things.

Those who use the sea to earn their daily bread are one of the best sources of information about the oceans. Captain Joseph Clydesdale, an Englishman, is just such a person. He skippers a deep-sea tug working out of Southampton. In Breira, Algeria, where his powerful vessel had just finished towing a huge bucket-dredge into the harbor, he said, "The ocean can be likened to the bloodstream in a human body. As it pulses throughout the framework of the earth, it does all sorts of magical things."

In this he is right. The ocean supplies the land with chemicals needed to nourish our farms, for rain generated over the sea is known to carry sixty-one different chemicals.

Rainfall also regulates our atmosphere, thereby controlling the temperature of the earth. It fills our reservoirs with drinking water. It stocks our rivers with flowing water that carries away our earthly waste. This sewage is dumped into the sea, where it is broken down by chemical reaction. After the water has been properly cleansed, it is again sucked into the skies and stored in black storm clouds that move over the land. Once inland, it is again dumped in the form of rain, which causes the process to start all over again.

It is far out at sea, in the very deep waters, that the real work is done. Here, in the area some scientists call "the stomach of the universe," all the solids washed off the earth are broken down. They are, in a sense, digested. During the process, they become edible food for fish and underwater plant life. Billions and billions of fish and other aquatic animals keep this rich food supply stirred up. If they did not fight among themselves and live violent lives, the nourishment would settle to the bottom. If that were to happen, our rain, taken off the top of the ocean, would become sterile. The blood supply of the world would turn anemic. Our crops would wither and die for lack of enrichment.

However, the sea cannot be examined in piecemeal fashion. To appreciate its vast size, one must study the entire globe. Let us simplify this large undertaking by reducing the oceans of the world into three great masses of water: The Pacific Ocean is the largest. The Atlantic is next in size. Then comes the Indian Ocean. The Arctic Ocean (at the North Pole) and the Antarctic Ocean (at the South Pole) are considered to be extensions of these.

The oceans of the world are really great reservoirs of heat. The water soaks up the warmth of the sun. Through circulation of currents, surface waves, and the flushing action of tides, this warm water is distributed around the world. The rise and fall of temperatures in the sea is far less than on land. The warmth of the ocean rarely goes above 80 degrees Fahrenheit. It seldom falls more than a few degrees below freezing.

Since the flow of water is away from the equator and toward either pole, the seas act as a giant weather machine. Or, if you prefer, an air conditioner for the entire world. The seas take in the heat of the tropics to lose it at colder latitudes. When chilled at either pole, by icebergs and glaciers, sea water is returned to cool the warmer latitudes. It keeps cities that are far removed from the equator from freezing and keeps our tropical cities from burning up. If it were not for this circulatory motion, Norway and Sweden would be blocks of ice. Cuba and Venezuela, burning infernos.

Of course, the temperatures decrease with depth. Bottom temperatures, in all latitudes, are about 32

This old print was made to illustrate what happens in the Indian Ocean. The crew of a wrecked vessel are being attacked by man-eating lobsters. PHOTOGRAPH COURTESY OF THE REX NAN KIVELL COLLECTION, NATIONAL LIBRARY OF AUSTRALIA, CANBERRA.

degrees Fahrenheit. The average depth of ocean water throughout the world is around 12,500 feet. To give some comparison, this is about the average height of our Rocky Mountains. The uneven sea floor is divided into basins by giant ridges. Large land masses, called continents, are bordered by shelves and slopes. These shelves are an important feature of the oceans.

To the eye of the landsman, the sea begins where water touches the visible ground. Quite often this is a beach or some other convenient spot from which to watch the waves. However, at the shore line the land gradually slopes downward into the sea. It is a shelf extending into the water and is, in fact, called the *continental shelf*. A shelf surrounds each continent. The average width of this shelf is 42 miles—of course it varies from one continent to

9

another. For instance, the shelf extends only one mile off the coast of California, but it runs out to about 800 miles along the north coast of Siberia.

At the edge of every shelf, there is a sharp drop. This is called a *continental slope*. It falls steeply to the floor of the ocean, which is known as the *abyssal depths*. These depths vary. They run from close to 24,442 feet (about 4½ miles) in the Indian Ocean, to 37,782 feet (about 8 miles) in the Pacific.

Features on the ocean bottom are similar to what we find on land. Each ocean is divided by continuous systems of mountains, the largest of these being the Mid-Atlantic Ridge. In the North Pacific an intermittent ridge lies in the west. So most of the deep sea floor is made up of basins surrounded by walls. Oceanographers sometimes compare the absolute floor of the ocean to the surface of the moon, because mountains also cover a great portion of the moon. Some of the lunar peaks, usually of circular formation, have an elevation of 26,000 feet. Amidst these mountains are thousands of craters, cracks, and caves. If this comparison is accurate, it is not hard to accept the following information released by the National Geographic Society. Of all living things on our globe, including plants as well as animals, four out of every five exist in the sea. And although one cannot be certain of the exact number, there are between 15,000 to 40,000 different species of fish. This includes the largest animal ever known to have existed on our globe, the blue whale. It is a creature of the deep that frequently measures over 100 feet in length.

So we see that the floor of the ocean is extremely uneven. The abyssal depths (also called the basin), the slope, and the shelf are all rutted. They are gouged by canyons, split by crevasses, bored out by tunnels, and laced with underground rivers. So there are plenty of places for sea monsters to hide at any level.

But it must be remembered that man knows very

little about the floor of the ocean. There is not enough light. As we all know, ocean water grows darker as the ground drops downward. Of course, how much light penetrates the water depends on how dirty it happens to be. So much mud is carried downstream by the Mississippi that at the mouth of the river, there is zero visibility below the surface of the water, while in some portions of the Pacific, it is possible to see fish 50 feet below.

When it comes to looking for sea monsters, the weight of water must also be considered. As we know, a

This old print shows why some sailors called large ocean beasts "sea monsters," while others called them "sea serpents," although both were seeing the same animal. There are plenty of places on the floor of the ocean where such animals could hide. PHOTOGRAPH COURTESY OF MARINERS MUSEUM, NEWPORT NEWS, VA.

bucket of water is heavy. On the floor of the Pacific the weight of water overhead is more than 16,300 pounds per square inch. A large elephant weighs only around 12,000 pounds, which means that a deep-sea diver would have at least one elephant standing on every inch of his body. Obviously, he would be squashed flat.

Through years of underwater exploration, man has established one thing for certain: in the black, cold depths of these unbearable pressures swim many forms of animal life. All are savage, grotesque, and suited to their cruel environment. Fortunately, those we know about are small. Unfortunately, there are probably many forms of animal life we do not even suspect exist. Nevertheless, it must be assumed that those yet to be discovered will be equally as odd-shaped, brutal, aggressive and monstrous. What we need now is not more theory but more exploration—just better ways of putting man on the absolute bottom of the ocean. This could take a great many years.

It is this pressure that makes it so difficult for man to reach the bottom of the sea. Let us consider this weight. As individuals living on the face of the earth, we are subject to certain atmospheric pressures. At sea level, air presses down on our bodies at 15 pounds per square inch. We do not feel this weight because the pressure within our bodies is the same as that on the outside. One pressure offsets the other. This amount of pressure, at sea level, is used as a standard of measurement. It is called "one atmosphere." Two atmospheres would be 30 pounds per square inch, three atmospheres would be 45, and so on.

However, if we go up, the amount of air over us becomes less. As a consequence, the weight becomes less. Therefore, in an airplane traveling at a great height, the cabin must be pressurized. This means that more weight must be added to the air within the cabin. This is much like pumping air into a tire. The internal pressure becomes greater than the external pressure.

An early English ship's captain described seeing this sea monster rise out of the depths. There are probably many such forms of animal life living in the depths of the sea. PHOTOGRAPH COURTESY OF MARINERS MUSEUM, NEWSPORT NEWS, VA.

The reverse of this is when we go down into the sea. Water weighs about 800 times more than air. Obviously, then, the deeper we go, the more weight will press against our bodies. So at the bottom of the deepest part in the Pacific reached by the Navy bathyscaphe (35,800 feet), the weight of water overhead was 1,086 atmospheres. Multiply this by 15 and the result is 16,290 pounds per square inch.

SEA MONSTERS

As has been previously stressed, darkness is another hindrance when man dives into the great depths. Although the content of ocean water varies throughout the world, it is generally conceded that light ends at about 600 feet. Beyond that depth, man's vision is zero. With electric lights, he might be able to see an additional 10 or 15 feet. Any number of large sea monsters, with excellent eyesight under such conditions, could be swimming just beyond the 15-foot range. Man would be completely unaware of their presence.

2

Some Big Ones
We Know About

EXAGGERATION is a well-publicized characteristic of fishermen. The "one that got away" is always so much larger than those at hand. This is not because truthful men become less truthful when they pick up a fishing rod. It is simply that emotions, such as surprise, shock, and fear, enter into any encounter with a big fish. To suddenly come face to face with a shark bigger than a man is a frightening experience. After the ordeal, the beast is often remembered as 24 feet long and "as big as a house."

Yet there are peculiarities about fish that at times become hard to accept. Take the familiar halibut, for example. It is a tasty fish that most sport fishermen are delighted to catch in sizes up to about 3 feet. Suddenly, a fisherman in a small offshore cabin cruiser hooks a 9-foot halibut. It probably weighs somewhere close to 1,000 pounds. He has to cut the fish loose, because so much weight would sink his small boat.

As the afterglow of pleasant surprise, shock, and terror drain out of the fisherman's system, his imagination goes to work. Being a landsman, the fisherman compares what was on his hook to animals with which he is familiar. A horse? Yes, it appeared to be as big as a good-sized stallion. Or a cow. Perhaps it was the size of a Hereford bull. Soon, in the fisherman's imagination, the halibut becomes a 2,000-pounder.

Yet there is no man alive who can officially set this fisherman straight. Even the experts can't agree on the size of the biggest halibut. Check a half dozen reference books and you will find as many different size limitations. Check with commercial fishermen and you will discover they catch them bigger than any listed in a textbook.

If this tendency to misjudge weight and size exists for the common halibut, think what happens when a shark is on the end of a line. It becomes massive and, certainly, monstrous. Obviously, people are apt to misjudge the size of certain large creatures of the sea. This in turn gives rise to sea monster stories.

In order to dispel such exaggerations, let us study a few of the unusual larger marine species and give the true facts as they are best known today.

Ribbonfish. These peculiar-looking fish are mentioned because they look like young sea monsters. They have a body that is very long and ribbon-shaped. The entire upper surface is topped by a large delicate fin. Its skin is naked of scales, its eyes are big. The mouth is toothless or possesses only weak teeth. The color is silvery with a bluish tinge. It grows to a length of somewhat over 20 feet. It has been known to weigh as much as 600 pounds. Upon occasion, one will be washed ashore, and then the excitement commences. Ribbonfish look like what most people think a sea monster *should* look like, so a captured one never fails to cause an uproar. Once hauled out of the water, these fish rapidly shrivel up and die. They lose their fierce look. The meat of the ribbonfish

Exaggeration is a well-publicized characteristic attributed to fisher-men. This seemed to be the case with Norwegian fishermen of the 1800s who said they were frequently bothered by this sea monster. PHOTO-GRAPH COURTESY OF NASJONALGALLERIET, OSLO, NORWAY.

17

is useless as food. In Scandinavia, where dogs live on fish, even they refuse to eat the flesh.

Mola. This name is Latin and means "millstone." It is certainly an accurate description of this fish. The body is oval-shaped, covered with leathery skin, and massive. They have been known to weigh 5 or 6 tons. The fish creates the appearance of a cartwheel 12 feet in diameter. The dorsal fin is very high. The mola has only a small mouth, which projects somewhat like a parrot's beak. The teeth are fused together to form a single, sharp plate in each jaw. These huge globs of fish are either a dirty brown or a drab gray.

The mola is sometimes called a headfish, because the roundness gives the effect of a big head without any body attached. They are also called sunfish, because they like to rise to the surface and bask in the sun. They live in the open sea, and on clear, warm days they rise to the surface, sprawl on their sides, and soak up the sun. When seen in this fashion, they have often been mistaken for some sort of a sea monster.

Little is known about the mola, for their meat is not good to eat. It is said to be tough and tasteless, and possesses parts that are known to be poisonous.

Giant Squid. This is a cigar-shaped beast that has an arrow-shaped upper part, large human-like eyes, and arms similar to those of an octopus. In fact, it belongs to the same scientific family as the octopus—the family of *cephalopods*. For sheer horror, ugliness, and savagery the giant squid is hard to beat. This is because, in addition to eight snakelike arms that twine around a victim, they have two tentacles capable of shooting out to grasp an object as far away as 50 to 90 feet. To make them even more dangerous, each tentacle is equipped with a catlike claw fitted with bony hooks.

Stories of massive, many-armed sea monsters attacking fishermen, boats, and even large ships are as old as history. Ancient Greek pottery depicts giant squids attacking boats. Japanese woodcuts show giant squids battling with a whale. Writers of the Roman era told of giant squid that reached aboard boats to snatch away sailors. However, because these dangerous beasts live along the bottom of the deep sea, little was then known about them. From time to time a dead one would be washed ashore. Or a whale and a giant squid locked in battle would rise to the surface of the ocean. Large whales relish these squid as food. They plunge to the bottom, grasp a giant squid in their jaws, and shoot to the surface for air. There, a furious battle takes place, with the whale generally winning.

On November 30, 1861, a French warship named the *Alecton* came upon a giant squid swimming on the surface of the ocean. For a time the ship's crew cannonaded the unknown animal. This seemed to have little or no effect, so they decided to try and haul it aboard. This too failed. Nevertheless, bringing the animal close inboard gave several officers an opportunity to study its size and shape. They later estimated it to weigh several tons and have tentacles so long they could not be fully measured. This was man's first opportunity to report accurately on the odd shape of these beasts.

At about the same time as the *Alecton* incident, no less than a dozen or more of these frightening monsters were stranded on the shores of Newfoundland. On October 26, 1873, a giant squid in Conception Bay, at the southeastern extremity of Newfoundland, attacked two fishermen in an open boat. The men struggled and finally succeeded in chopping off one of the beast's arms to make their escape. Based on this single piece of the animal brought ashore, scientists estimated the giant squid to have had arms 33 feet long.

One scientist of the period, A. C. Oudemans, wrote that he had measured giant squid with arms 90 feet long.

Furthermore, he had measured scars appearing on harpooned whales and estimated that some squids could have claws that were fitted to arms at least 120 feet long. To have a beast of this size come climbing aboard your boat would be a horrifying experience.

Green Moray Eel. The eel is one of the most plentiful fish in the sea. It is snakelike in appearance but scaleless, and unlike the snake it does have teeth. The green moray is not only the largest of eels (it grows to 10 or 12 feet in length) but also the most vicious. These eels are found throughout warmer waters of the world. Their powerful muscles, tough skin, and strong jaws make them very dangerous. Green morays have the ability to strike with great speed and deadly accuracy. Their flesh is poisonous.

Some large eels possess the unique ability to breathe through gills while under water. They can absorb oxygen through their flesh when burrowed into mud. Or they can rise to the surface and breathe air. To see a large green moray on the surface of the ocean is unusual. They live among coral on the bottom of the sea and come out to hunt at night. Occasionally, one is forced to rise to the surface during hours of daylight. Instantly, the cry goes up. Sea serpent! Indeed, to watch a green moray swimming through the water is a frightening sight. They are mean-looking, grouchy, and easily aroused.

Natives of the Fiji Basin, in the South Pacific, say they occasionally see a type of green moray that is 20 or more feet long. They also say it is best avoided. It supposedly attacks canoes whenever it encounters them on the surface, but fortunately this rarely happens, since the eel generally remains hidden in coral caves deep in the water.

Giant Devil Ray. Ray fishes are flat, with eyes on the upper surfaces of their bodies. Most rays are noted for their poisonous tails. The devil ray, or manta, is different. It is known for its bulk. Some attain a width of 30 feet and weigh 4,000 or more pounds. These devil rays are dangerous only because of their size. Helmet divers, using air hoses and safety lines, find them extremely alarming. Being powerful swimmers and curious by nature, they are inclined to dart through a stream of air bubbles. Their fins, or wings, become entangled in the lines, and in short order the diver's helmet is ripped loose and he drowns.

These huge rays like to bask just under the surface of the water. They leave the tips of their fins protruding into the air. People frequently mistake so much living bulk as belonging to none other than a sea monster.

3

What Is
a Sea Monster?

T HE dictionary defines a sea monster as "any large or unusual sea animal." Almost as a footnote, it adds, "Often represented as man-eating."

Father Neptune, believed by ancient Greeks to be god of the seas, would get a laugh out of this description. For the oceans of the world are abundant with massive, big-toothed, irritable animals that are both willing and able to gobble down a man.

"Furthermore," says Captain Otter Cosalt, an old Scottish merchant seaman, "if you haven't as yet found a beast big enough, or ornery enough, to suit your idea of a sea monster, just you wait awhile. The sea is always concocting new animals that no one has ever seen before."

Captain Cosalt should know. He is a master mariner who retired after more than forty years at sea. He likes to point out that the sea offers great possibilities for revealing new monsters. It is the nursery for all living things. It is the backyard from which came dinosaurs and giant prehistoric reptiles. It still harbors the octopus, the whale, the tiger shark, and the piranha. It keeps hidden from our view such strange suborders as the deep-sea muzzlefish, which is long, slender, and horribly ugly; the giant cuttlefish, a massive ten-armed beast; the gulper eel—a snakelike fish that is almost all mouth; the deep-sea devilfish—so ugly it defies description; and many others.

It is also the home of the true sea serpents. One of these sea serpents, the anaconda snake of South America,

Some mariners claim that the sea still offers great possibilities for revealing new monsters. It is the nursery for all living things. From these waters came dinosaurs and giant prehistoric reptiles. Abnormalities among marine species could again produce a sea serpent such as that depicted by Paul Gustave Doré in 1873. PHOTOGRAPH COURTESY OF LE CLERC, PARIS, FRANCE.

is a marine animal that grows to a length of 40 feet, and is wide of girth. At times it becomes very aggressive. Then there is also the seagoing crocodile of the South Pacific. It will reach 15 feet in length and is very vicious. It has jaws so powerful they can snap a man in two.

Is it possible that the ocean is also the home of some amphibious dinosaurs that escaped extinction by returning to the sea? Recorded sea monster sightings, made

23

millions of years later, describe creatures possessing a strange resemblance to reptiles that lived during the Mesozoic era, which began nearly 230 million years ago.

Geologists have uncovered the remains of dinosaurs. Since many of their bones are encased in rock or preserved in permafrost beyond the Arctic Circle, we have a definite record of what these land-based animals looked like. Unfortunately, man has not as yet been able to explore the floor of the ocean fully. All we can do is look at the great beasts that once trod the earth and guess at how they compare with those in the sea.

Let us assume for a moment that you have been carried back 200 million years and dropped somewhere on planet Earth. To begin with, there would be no other human beings. You would be the only person in the entire world. Now you are on your own. Look about you carefully.

Notice the ground. It is soft and mushy. It is not quite swampland as we know it today, but it is not far from it. There are no trees in this weird land, but there are forests of a sort—forests made up of giant ferns, many of them resembling palm trees. Grass does not grow on the ground. Instead, there is a thick undergrowth of smaller ferns.

When you stop to listen, there is only silence, for there are no singing birds, no honeybees buzzing from flower to flower. Just mile after mile of green ferns. The air is hot and steamy. Rain clouds roll in, low, black, and threatening. Hidden amidst all of this are great bugs, for this is a large, new world and everything about it is massive. There are spiders as long as the palm of your hand. There are deadly scorpions as long as your foot. There are dragonflies with wings 18 to 30 inches from tip to tip. Giant cockroaches are everywhere. They scurry among the ferns, crawl the length of the palms, and fly from one high spot to another.

The sea is not far away. It is never far away. Always,

its waves can be heard beating against the shores. When the winds commence to howl, as they often do, the land becomes flooded. This does not bother the great beasts that populate this strange world. They have enormous round bellies to help them float when the land floods. They have large feet that enable them to walk on mushy ground. And many have long periscope-like necks that permit them to go into the sea and gobble down schools of fish.

Overhead there are flying reptiles. These are not birds. They have no feathers and their wings are covered with a leathery skin. They are massive beasts with long hooked beaks and horribly sharp claws. Many are the size of a stout Shetland pony, with wings that are 10 to 12 feet long. They swoop about, snatching at smaller reptiles

Plesiosaurs (left) and icthyosaurs were two of the marine animals that are thought to have died out over 100 million years ago. The plesiosaurs were reptile-like. They had a long neck and a rudder-like tail. The head was long and armed with strong teeth. Icthyosaurs were fishlike in form and had four paddles for limbs, a long muzzle, and a great number of big teeth. PHOTOGRAPH COURTESY OF THE FIELD MUSEUM OF NATURAL HISTORY, CHICAGO, ILL.

skittering among the ferns. Others fly far out to sea and drop down to grab fish in their powerful talons.

Dominating this peculiar world of constant turmoil is water. There are lakes, streams, creeks, puddles, marshes, and almost constant rain. Then, above all, there is the sea that surrounds all of the land. Everyone of the reptiles seems able to cope with it. They can walk on it, swim in it, hide in it, and eat from it. All recognize it as a source of food and a place of safety.

Not complete safety, just safety against dangerous things that cause panic on land. Things like lightning and fire. Not safety against other mighty lizards that live in the sea. Certainly not safety against sharks with cavernous mouths.

Still, many dinosaurs were well equipped to combat such attackers. They were big and strong. They could swim. They had fiercely sharp teeth and powerful jaws and could hold their breath for long periods. In a sense, they were perfectly fitted to live in the sea.

This was still a tropical sort of world. It was forever encased in fog, shrouded in fumes, and stricken with oppressive humidity. It was ideal for dinosaurs, amphibians, reptiles, and fish. Especially for fish. They found new depths to explore. New places to hide were constantly being opened to them, while food was more than plentiful. They fought with one another, propagated, gorged themselves, and grew enormous.

Then came a change. Dinosaurs disappeared. What brought about their disappearance, no one can say for sure, but we do know that when they went, they went quickly. After millions upon millions of years, these egg-laying beasts, which ranged up to 90 feet in length, were gone. It was not as if one species, such as the dog or the house cat, were to disappear. This was a whole order, suborder, family, subfamily, and genus that disappeared. Nor was it as if a local plague had wiped clean just one large area. Whatever it was that killed them was universal. It was worldwide.

About 100 million years ago, the sea looked like this. Giant turtles, giant birds, giant lizards, and giant fish—everything was big. To survive, an animal had to have plenty of size. Not much of a brain was needed, just speed and powerful jaws. PHOTOGRAPH COURTESY OF THE FIELD MUSEUM OF NATURAL HISTORY, CHICAGO, ILL.

Fossil remains of dinosaurs have been found in rock strata of every continent. These remains show that dinosaurs differed widely in body structure, in the type of location in which they lived, and in their diet. Their intelligence, judged by the size of their brain cavities, was low; they were stupid beasts, motivated by instinct. But these instincts had been powerful enough to protect them for over 100 million years. Had this hereditary aptitude suddenly deserted them? Or was this driving instinct powerful enough that some amphibious dinosaurs, living on the fringe of the sea, managed to escape from an unknown peril into the watery depths?

The oceans of the world did not suffer from the same blight that struck the land. There is no record of a universal fish kill. The whale is proof that massive beasts could and do exist in the sea. The great white shark demonstrates that fish with a low mentality, guided mostly by a strong instinct, continued as ever before.

27

SEA MONSTERS

Can science guess at what happened to the dinosaurs? Yes, of course. Some interesting theories have been offered. A combination of factors, such as geographic and climatic changes, seems to be the most logical reason. Volcanic action greatly altered the surface of the world. The crust of the world took on a new shape. Swamps—the happy home of dinosaurs throughout the world—drained away. Mountains created colder climates. Dinosaurs could not survive in the cooler temperatures.

In addition, some were wiped out by excessive floods. Others could not compete with smaller, swifter mammals that were becoming increasingly numerous. Lastly, the herbs and plants of the era, on which dinosaurs depended for their great bulk, changed. Ferns became less plentiful. They also became smaller in size. Trees, flowers, mountains, snow, sleet, and other scenic transformations took place. It was a new world.

But similar alterations did not take place in the sea. Water is much more constant than air. Its temperature varies little when compared with land temperatures. In the ocean depths plant life is not the major source of food. Fish eat other fish for nourishment, so life remained less alterable in the sea. Because of these factors, the oceans of the world could have offered sanctuary to the hard-pressed amphibians.

Who can say that none now hide on the floor of the ocean? Especially since so little is known about the bottom of the sea.

Captain Cosalt suggests another explanation for sea monsters: Changes in ocean temperatures may cause extraordinary changes in sea life, just as climatic shifts on land affect plants and animals. As on land, there are many different climates beneath the surface of the ocean. On land people accept certain facts about the atmosphere. They understand that the air in Brazil is hotter than the air in Alaska. People also agree that temperatures are lower at the North Pole than at the equator. These same variations exist in the sea—only more so. Changes are caused by water pressure, the presence or lack of light, and the rise and fall of tides. There are also currents that must be considered. Some run along the surface of the sea. Some are deep down and sweep across the floor of the ocean.

"On land," the Captain says, "we have animal life that can stand extreme heat. An example of this is the kangaroo rat. This tiny creature does fine in temperatures running as high as 150 degrees. It lives in Death Valley, California. There you find one of the hottest and driest climates on earth."

He explains that many people are curious about what even a tiny rat can find to eat in so barren a wasteland. "Let me tell you about a radical change that took place in Death Valley. It came about during May of 1939. In that land where there is never any rain, they suddenly experienced showers every day for half that month.

"So what happened? Seeds that had been buried in the ground for centuries received water for the first time. They sprouted into life. Funny-looking bugs also came into being. Both insects and plant life were odd-shaped and wrinkled in appearance. The rats never had it so good. They ate too well. In no time at all they grew big bellies. If the rain had continued, they too would have quickly sprouted into large grotesque animals.

"Now let us say the same sort of thing takes place in the darkest part of the ocean. A small, ugly-shaped fish is suddenly exposed to sunlight. Changes in current surround it with warm, nourishing water. The animal spreads. It grows huge. Suddenly it rises to the surface of the ocean. Now it is a massive, disfigured beast. Those of us who see it are frightened.

"This sea monster, like those things blooming in Death Valley, soon dies. It leaves no trace of its presence. Those who say they saw it are laughed at. No one can find any such beast in the sea."

SEA MONSTERS

Captain Cosalt shrugs. "So how can I, or any other man, accurately describe a sea monster? What we see today is not what we are apt to see tomorrow. We can be sure that nature creates hideous monsters. But where they come from, where they disappear to, or what they look like, no one can say for certain."

Dr. Anthony Blair, an oceanographer and a graduate of the famous French *Institut Océanographique*, who now serves as an adviser to the United States fishing industry, partially agrees with the captain. But "he oversimplifies the matter," says Dr. Blair. "When people speak of a sea monster, they generally have in mind a long, snakelike beast. This animal shows loops as it moves through the water and has a big head, fiery eyes, and a large mouth fitted with fangs. Things like that just don't grow as rapidly as the captain suggests. Nor, for that matter, do they always die as quickly."

He offers a third explanation for sea monsters. "What causes a massive animal to appar on the surface of the ocean is no doubt the result of *mutation*. This word means that the offspring differs from its parents in some well-marked way. Generally, we call them 'freaks.' As an example, here on earth we have a certain number of cows and chickens born with two heads. These freaks of nature seldom live for very long.

"Fish and other marine life are of a lower order than barnyard animals. As a result, mutations happen more often. Also, they can be caused much more easily. A sudden change in conditions surrounding a marine organism may bring about a mutation. This could give rise to a freak fish, or a sea serpent. Thusn we have a perfect example of the true sea monster."

The doctor believes that these undersea freaks generally do not live too long either. Furthermore, they cannot reproduce more of their own image. Hence, when a big hairy beast is seen gliding across the surface of the ocean, it might be the only one of a kind. Furthermore, this young scientist believes that mutations, freaks, sea monsters, or whatever else one might call them, happen frequently.

"Man himself is the cause of this," Dr. Blair says. "He is forever dumping chemicals into the sea. These chemicals pollute the ocean. Poisons surround the fish. Biological changes then take place within the parent fish. The offspring are sometimes grotesque. They become horrid-looking things that grow heads too big for their bodies. Or even large disfigured bodies that are too big for tiny heads.

"We have learned," the doctor says, "that a poison most of us call 'mustard gas' causes mutations in sea life. Changes in marine animals can be induced through use of this chemical. Actually, this so-called 'gas' is a colorless, oily compound (carbon, hydrogen, chlorine, and sulfur). In sea water it remains concentrated.

"On the 18th of August, 1970, our government intentionally sank the old Liberty ship S.S. *Briggs*. It was loaded with 2,664 tons of army chemicals, including mustard gas. The hull rests at a depth of 16,000 feet, not far from Daytona Beach. How do we know those chemicals are not leaking into the sea to create horrible sea monsters?"

It is true that the government used the floor of the ocean as a dumping ground for its unwanted poison gases. Regardless of what care is taken, someday, if not today, a container will leak. Sea water will eventually eat its way through anything. Given five, ten, twenty-five, or even a thousand years, the sea will rot away the strongest of materials. Then, slowly, a leak. It will be like opening a cage to let loose a countless army of sea monsters.

"That ship holds other gases," Dr. Blair adds. "Some far worse than mustard gas. There is one gas that contains plague germs. This germ killed 25 million people during the fourteenth century. There are also botulism germs out there. This is a form of food poisoning 2 thousand times more deadly than mustard gas.

"Suppose a huge sea monster suddenly appears in

31

SEA MONSTERS

New York harbor. It disrupts ship traffic. It causes a great deal of damage along the waterfront. Marine police rush onto the scene and machine-gun the animal. When it is dead, countless sightseers crawl all over the carcass to take pictures. Television men from all over the country crowd aboard to get the best angle. After a few days, the dead animal is towed to sea and blown up with dynamite."

The incident is forgotten. But several weeks later, people in widespread parts of the nation become violently ill. They break out with ugly sores, cough up blood, and die. Doctors rush to conduct post-mortems. They find, to their horror, that these people died of the plague.

Commercial fishermen have their own ideas about what a sea monster is. These hard-working, tough-minded men are found in every seaport in the world.

Captain Peter Giacola is the skipper of the 228-foot tuna-fishing boat *Lucky Lady*. His vessel is large for a fishing boat. It goes to sea for many days at a time and is built to live through the roughest of storms. Its home port is Tacoma, Washington.

"I've seen 'em," he answers promptly. "Our nets have come up with sea monsters a landsman wouldn't believe. Some are round of body, hairy, and long. We don't fool with them. We shoot 'em quick with a heavy-caliber rifle. They can rip up an expensive net in a matter of minutes."

On the far side of the globe, a Japanese fisherman named Tsugii Hatami captains a whale killer. This is a small ship that works in Japan's Antarctic whaling fleet. It has a harpoon gun mounted on the bow. It fires a shell that explodes after penetrating the whale. This kills the whale and expands barbs into its body.

"I cannot say for sure what a sea monster looks like," the captain says. "However, I do know they exist."

How does he know this?

"One morning we were drifting through a heavy mist. The lookout suddenly yells there is a whale off our

32

starboard bow. It is my good fortune to be on the bridge. So I grab a pair of binoculars and look. Sure enough, out there, floating quietly on the surface, is something big. Looks like the biggest whale I have ever seen.

"Then *bang* goes our gun. By all the holiness of Raijin [god of thunder], we had a ryu [water dragon] on the line. It reared high over the bow. Then it reached out with clawlike fins and began to climb aboard. The gunner was killed. His assistant cut the line. I put the engine at full astern. We parted company with the ryu. It was all over within seconds."

For every deep-sea fisherman presented with the question "What is a sea monster?" there is a different answer. None denies the fact that such beasts exist, but no two can agree on what they are.

A Greek fisherman believes they are overgrown fish, like the mola which normally grows to about 10 feet long and weighs close to 2,000 pounds. He believes a freak mola will sometimes grow to twice that length and twice that weight.

A French fisherman says a sea monster is an awfully big grouper or rockfish. He says that he has seen one of these fish that weighed 1,000 pounds and was close to 10 feet long.

Many commercial fishermen name one or another kind of shark as being the true sea monster. "We do not know as yet how big sharks grow," says an Australian fisherman. "Big devils we have caught. How big is the biggest, no one can say."

Which just about answers the question "What is a sea monster?" In truth, no one can say for certain. They are underwater monstrosities—that's all we know.

4

The Fish That Wouldn't Stay Dead

IN previous chapters we have seen how the oceans, the
earth, and the animals on this planet all changed.
These alterations took billions and billions of years.
During these ages some sea animals became land animals; some land animals then became sea animals. And
some animals seemed to be midway in making a change
from one to the other.

Two such species that lived during the Cretaceous
period—135 to 70 million years ago—were a fish and a
long-necked marine reptile. The fish was called a coelacanth (pronounced seé-lah-canth); the reptile, an *elasmosaurus* (pronounced e-laz-mo-sawŕ-us). The fish
seemed to have been evolving toward a life on shore, for
it had commenced to grow legs. The reptile had no
trouble sampling life on firm ground. But the coelacanth
halted its move to the shore, and the elasmosaurus made
its home in the sea, always within easy reach of the moist
soil.

Because it remained in ocean waters, the coelacanth
developed thick, armor-plated sides. It also developed
large jaws and long fanglike teeth. For speed in the

water and safety against enemies, it grew to a length of about 7 feet.

The elasmosaurus was the length of about three modern automobiles. Being fitted with a long neck, a small head, and rows of sharp teeth, it was faced with fewer enemies. Life for this beast was less of a struggle than it was for the coelacanth. On good days, when luck was running favorably, it might even succeed in snatching a small coelacanth out of the sea.

Nevertheless, the coelacanth prospered. It became the most numerous fish in the sea. It spread throughout the world. It more than held its own against the larger elasmosauras and others of the dinosaurs.

Then, suddenly, something happened throughout the entire world. Fish in the sea changed; animals on land changed; bugs, insects, and birds changed. The big beasts of the sea disappeared. Animal life became smaller. Flowers bloomed. The world took on a certain loveliness. Somewhere in what we now call Africa, apelike men appeared. The savage coelacanth receded, became scarce, disappeared.

Millions of years later, modern man researched the land and found the fossilized remains of the elasmosaurus. He researched the bottom of the sea and discovered the fossilized bones of the coelacanth. Laboratory tests proved that the elasmosaurus and the coelacanth had lived somewhat parallel lives. Both could be traced back further than the Devonian period—400 million to 300 million years ago. They had coexisted during the Cretaceous period and become extinct at its conclusion, 70 million years ago.

But a peculiar thing happened. A live coelacanth was brought to the surface of the sea! This occurred in a rather roundabout manner.

On December 22, 1938, a commercial fishing boat was trawling off the small village of East London, in the Union of South Africa. The vessel was 160 feet long and what seamen call a "stern trawler for middle water," which meant that nets were lowered over the after end and towed at depths anywhere between the surface of the sea and the bottom of the ocean. It was a beautiful day, with little or no wind, and the crew looked forward to a good catch.

"Lower the nets to forty fathoms," Captain Goosen ordered his men. At 240 feet, they stood an excellent chance of netting a fat catch. The little vessel cruised slowly back and forth. She was about 3 to 5 miles off shore. The nets began to drag against the pull of the propeller. That meant a good catch had been netted.

"Haul in the net," the captain ordered. "All hands stand by to sort fish."

When the trawl was inboard, the catch was dumped on deck.

The crew cheered for almost three tons of plump fish tumbled across the deck. Crewmen began to sort the good fish from what is called "trash fish," inedible fish that are thrown back into the sea.

"Hey cap'n," one crewman called. "Is this big fish good to eat, or is it trash?"

Not daring to get too close, the captain inspected the thrashing fish. It was a peculiar-looking thing. In his thirty-two years at sea, Captain Goosen had never seen the likes of such a fish. It was about 7 feet long, heavy, and steel blue in color. Its sides were armor-plated with thick scales and it had large blue eyes. When the captain reached out to grab it by the tail, the fish jackknifed and snapped its jaws. The teeth were long, ragged-looking and sharp. The quick movement almost caught the skipper's hand. If it had, those teeth could have chopped off a few fingers.

It was almost four hours before the fish began to lose strength. It was indeed a very hardy species. Finally Captain Goosen was able to get close for a detailed examination. Unable to say what it was, he announced a decision.

"Men," he said, "we'll take this fish to Miss Latimer."

All hands agreed this was the thing to do. Miss Latimer was curator of East London's museum. Although it was only a small museum, there wasn't a fisherman on the coast of Africa who didn't know about Miss Latimer.

"She's everywhere," said the skipper of a 240-ton trawler named *Helen V.* "Whenever we land a haul, that young woman is on hand to look over the catch."

Which was true. Miss Latimer was trying her best to educate every skipper along the coast. She was forever telling them, "Don't throw any peculiar-looking fish away. Save them for me."

She even had information sheets printed. These she passed out to officers and men of the fishing fleet. Now her interest in the sea was about to pay off. Captain Goosen handed over his 130-pound fish to Miss Latimer. She studied it carefully for some time.

"I don't know what it is," she finally admitted. "But it is some rare species of lungfish."

Regardless of what it had been, it was now beginning to stink. This fish had been dead a long time. Something had to be done to preserve it. Miss Latimer decided to have a taxidermist mount the fish, but unfortunately the taxidermist threw away the insides of the fish. However, Miss Latimer made a series of sketches and sent them to the ichthyologist Dr. J. L. B. Smith. That gentleman hurried to East London for a look at the mounted fish. He was cautious about announcing any conclusion. It could all be a clever hoax. After all, neither he nor Miss Latimer had actually seen the fish alive. However, the two went over the remains of the fish time and time again. They discussed it between themselves. Dr. Smith was in a difficult spot. For over one hundred years famous scientists had been saying that the coelacanth was extinct. Now he, a man little known in the world of science, was about to say that this was not so. He hesitated.

"What type of fish did Captain Goosen find?" a local news reporter wanted to know. Fishermen had been talking. Several newspapers and radio stations had heard about the catch.

Dr. Smith personally interviewed everyone who had touched, or even seen, the peculiar fish when it was alive. This took time. The reporters were getting impatient. Erroneous reports were beginning to appear in the newspapers. Scientists from around the African continent began to call on the phone. They had questions needing answers. Dr. Smith decided to make a public announcement.

"This fish," he said, "had indeed been a live coelacanth."

The scientific world exploded. What nonsense! A fish from the Devonian period, 400 million to 350 million years ago, still alive? Impossible! Newspaper photographers, radio broadcasters, and newsreel cameramen swarmed into the little town of East London. To both Dr. Smith and Miss Latimer, so much attention was unwelcome. In truth, they did not have scientific proof that this species of fish was still alive.

Since it is known that animal life must exist in pairs, Dr. Smith set out to find the companion fish of Captain Goosen's coelacanth. He, like Miss Latimer, began to haunt the fishing docks. Fishing boat captains were shown pictures. They were given instructions on what to do and who to call if such a fish were ever caught. Nothing came of it. Captain Goosen's catch was believed to be a fake. Scientists still taught that the coelacanth had become extinct, along with dinosaurs, at the end of the Cretaceous period, about 70 million years ago.

World War II intervened, and the attempt to find a live coelacanth was abandoned. But after the war was over, Dr. Smith resumed his search. Several scientific agencies lent assistance. Fishermen were again called upon. Pictures were distributed. "If Captain Goosen's fish was caught in these waters," Dr. Smith reasoned, "others must be close by."

In 1952, fourteen years after the original catch by

The coelacanth shown here was supposed to have become extinct 70 million years ago. In December 1938, off the coast of a village called East London, in South Africa, a fishing boat hauled one up from the depths. It is now called "the living fossil," and many more have been caught in recent years. PHOTOGRAPH COURTESY OF BOB WILLIAMS, BUREAU OF COMMERCIAL FISHERIES, U.S. DEPARTMENT OF THE INTERIOR.

Captain Goosen, a wireless message was received. A ship's captain named Eric Hunt had caught a 5-foot coelacanth. He was saving it for Dr. Smith. The doctor raced off to find and board that ship. After many difficulties, he at last stood on the deck of Captain Hunt's vessel. There, before his eyes, was a coelacanth that had been alive only a few days before. It was perfectly preserved. The flesh was firm, the entrails had not been touched, the skin was unbroken, the scales were in good order, and the fins were in excellent shape. Here was positive proof. The coelacanth did exist.

To further support this fact, a well-known French institute of scientific research also received an uninjured specimen of a coelacanth. This happened just a short time after Dr. Smith's historic find. Then a group of French scientists recovered three more coelacanths. To celebrate this fact, the Musée d'Histoire Naturelle, of Paris, published a book on the subject of living coelacanths.

SEA MONSTERS

The news world exploded into headlines. Writers drew their own conclusions. If this fish, they reasoned, had succeeded in hiding along the floor of the ocean for millions of years, then certainly the elasmosaurus also could have made it. After all, the elasmosaurus was a more rugged creature. And if that long-necked animal were found to be alive, then sea monsters would exist for sure.

Newspapers, magazines, and that new medium, television, were in full cry. Sea monsters are real, they said.

During May of 1977 a rare event occurred. The captain of a Russian oceanographic ship consented to make a public statement about sea monsters. This was an unusual happening. Russian officials generally refuse to be put on record as having said anything on any subject. Nevertheless, Captain Mikhail Volsky, master of the *Dmitzy Mendelejer*, a 407-foot vessel with 28 scientific laboratories, had this to say while his ship was at anchor in Leningrad harbor:

"There is strong proof that the deep sea is a hiding place for animals that flourished in ancient times. They withdrew to the depths because they could not compete in crowded areas along the shore. The coelacanth proves this. We have to go deep to find them. However, the coelacanth is not the only ancient fish caught in the depths. There is the *Vampiroteuthis infernalis*. It is a strange creature that resembles an octopus and looks like a giant squid, but is neither. Now it is called a living fossil, for it was long ago declared extinct.

"Also, there is the shellfish called *Neopilina galathea*. This seems to be part snail and part clam. Scientists said that this animal became extinct about 350 million years ago. Regardless, we have now been catching them at depths of about 12,000 feet.

"My government has declared that about 20 percent of fish caught in depths over 15,000 feet are what we call "archaic." So we are certain that in the depths there are many strange beasts yet to be discovered. A number of these we very likely will term sea monsters."

Present day scientists no longer laugh at statements of this kind. After all, if the coelacanth could manage the survival trick, why not others? Or perhaps fifty or sixty others?

No doubt about it. The fish that wouldn't stay dead has taught the world a lot.

5

Some Early Reports of Sea Monsters . . .

E VER since man first began recording history, there have been stories about sea monsters. Myths, legends, sagas, fables and fairy tales have all been used to tell about one or another powerful beast that lived in the sea.

In the *Iliad*, written before 700 B.C., the Greek poet Homer had this to say about Poseidon, the god of the seas, and his underwater world: "Poseidon came to his palace in the depths of the ocean. There he harnessed three horses to his golden chariot. They were swift runners, with manes of golden hair. He caught up his whip of wrought gold. Then he set out over the waves. The monsters of the deep knew him well. They gamboled about him on all sides."

Centuries later, Scandinavian seamen were recording the activities of sea monsters. Since fishing was a major occupation in Norway, Sweden, and Denmark, a great number of the menfolk spent most of their lives afloat. From these maritime people came the word *kraken*, meaning "a monster of the sea." The word can be

From the earliest of man's history there have been stories about mermaids and mermen who lured passing ships onto the rocks. Generally, they were evil people, half-human, half-fish. PHOTOGRAPH COURTESY OF RIJKSMUSEUM, LEIDEN, HOLLAND.

traced back into Scandinavian mythology. By A.D. 1000, it was used to indicate a huge beast much like an octopus or giant squid.

Captain Axel Carlekrantz, who lives on the north bank of the Ljusnan River, in Söderhamn, Sweden, is active in the Society for Preservation of Old Ships. He has a document found aboard one ancient vessel. It reads in part: "Kraken has struck again. Seaman from nearby village of Skeljeskor was fishing with good sufficiency in waters near the 100-fathom bank off our shores. Our nets were heavy with cod and ling. Suddenly the fish are gone and we know then of the presence of the kraken. In haste, most of the fleet erect sails and turn for home. Some remain to do more fishing."

The document concludes that one Sture Dohnhammer, who owned a boat from Skellefte District, and his helper, named Holger, were both found dead two days

43

SEA MONSTERS

later. Their boat had been smashed and was half sunk. It was rumored that the kraken was guilty of this act.

As if to prove these rumors true, another report came to light. A man named Van Vlissingen, of Den Helder, in the Netherlands, was driven ashore in Sweden. Because he was a foreigner, not many people believed what he had to say. Nevertheless, he publicly took an oath by the Pope and the beard of good Saint Alban that he was nearby when Sture Dohnhammer was killed. He claimed that a two-horned kraken came out of the sea, rammed the man's boat, and ate the crew. Since the man was a stranger, he was "proclaimed a falsifyer."

During the following centuries, larger ships were built. Freighters, fishing vessels, and warships were all venturing farther over the horizons. In 1268 King Louis IX of France was given a ship by the city of Venice. It was supposed to be the largest merchant ship in the world—108 feet long, carrying a crew of a hundred and

"The kraken has struck again," became a common saying among early sailors. Here is shown what happens to a ship when it is attacked by a kraken, or giant squid. Many sailing ships were supposed to have been lost to these giant octopuses. PHOTOGRAPH COURTESY OF THE FORBES COLLECTION, MASSACHUSETTS INSTITUTE OF TECHNOLOGY.

ten men. It must have been a very crowded ship. Many modern tankers, the size of a football field, carry only thirty or forty crewmen.

But the king's new ship, and others soon to follow, allowed men to explore. The bigger the ships, the farther afield men traveled. And with increased travel came an increase in the number of sea monster stories brought ashore by crewmen. Tales of beasts so large they were mistaken for islands were frequent. Sometime before the close of the fifteenth century, Saint Brendan, a missionary from Ireland, is said to have alighted on a fish named Sasconye. It was so big and so kindly, according to the stories, that it held still while the holy man celebrated mass. After the ceremony, the saint returned to his ship and the monster descended again to the depths of the sea.

World exploration was forcefully brought to public attention by the voyages of Christopher Columbus and Vasco da Gama. In 1499 Vasco da Gama concluded a voyage that had taken him around the Cape of Good Hope, up the eastern coast of Africa to Malindi, and across the Indian Ocean to ancient Calicut. Calicut was once the leading seaport in Southern India but declined in influence during the nineteenth century. Nevertheless, this voyage opened up a trade route to the Indies. It also harvested a number of new stories about sea monsters.

A library in the Portuguese city of Figueira da Foz has the frayed remnants of a diary kept by a sailor. It is thought that the crewman was an officer on one of da Gama's ships. His name was Manoul de Sousa Barbara. In part, he wrote, "It is the dark that now frightens the men. Upon one instance, a stout fellow, tending the ship's tiller, was heard to scream. By the time another of the hands got to him and lanterns were aglow, he was gone. Only blood remained on deck. Others of our group then swore they had seen a long-haired beast following in our wake for two nights past. To balk further attack, we have placed a second man alongside the tillerman during times of intense darkness."

SEA MONSTERS

Olaus Magnus, a chartmaker with an imagination, was the first to draw pictures of ferocious-looking animals on early navigation charts. Then, to justify the pictures, he took to writing about weird beasts. Since Olaus was the brother of a Swedish Archbishop, his words were taken as gospel. In 1555 he published a book. His writings stated that people who sailed along the shores of

Frayed diaries and ancient records reveal that charts, such as this fragment of 1511, were used by navigators to plot a course across open seas. The figure warns of a mermaid that might appear to misdirect them. PHOTOGRAPH COURTESY OF THE MARITIME MUSEUM, HAIFA, ISRAEL.

Norway told of a strange sea animal. They related that a sea serpent more than 200 feet long and 20 feet thick lived in rocks and holes along the shores of Bergen. "It comes out," the book said, "only on summer nights to devour calves, lambs, and hogs. Or it goes into the seas to eat cuttles, lobsters, and sea crabs." Magnus said that it had hair two feet long hanging from its neck, sharp

46

scales, and flaming eyes. It attacked boats and snatched away crewmen.

The early years of the eighteenth century marked the birth of modern science. Great advances were made in all the disciplines: chemistry, physics, medicine, and biology. Mathematics was developed and refined. Men of learning were listened to and honored. One such scholar was Carolus Linneaus (1707-1778), a native of Sweden. He was the son of a minister. He graduated from

Swedish sailors told of a sea monster that was 200 feet long and 20 feet thick. It was said to live among the rocks along the shores of Bergen.
PHOTOGRAPH COURTESY OF THE NAVY LIBRARY, WASHINGTON, D.C.

university and later studied medicine and became a doctor. During his life he wrote and had published one hundred eighty books. By his own admission, he was a firm believer in sea monsters and sea serpents.

Linneaus is unusual in sea monster history. He is the only man on record who speaks well of sea monsters. He wrote that they helped the fleets locate fish and fill their nets because they caused unnatural shallows. However, he wrote, if the water suddenly turned even more shallow under one of the boats, it meant the kraken was coming up from the bottom. It marked a time when the fishing fleet should leave the area. His description of one such animal reads like this:

"Its upper part appears to be about an English mile and a half in circumference (some say more, but I choose the least). It looks like a number of small islands. At least several horns appear ... and sometimes they stand as high as the masts of middle-sized vessels. It seems these are the arms. They say that if they were to lay hold of the largest man of war they would pull it to the bottom."

The discussion about krakens and their size grew intense. Many politicians expressed a view. In the eighteenth century, one was Rugebregt, the Harbor Master of Alkmaar, in the Netherlands. His status was equivalent to that of a present-day mayor, or city manager. He wrote: "Myself, I have seen kraken, round of head, big of eye, fierce in appearance. They have arms that extend beyond the length of our biggest ship. At night, should one of our vessels be anchored in the outer harbor, they crawl aboard. Once on board, their arms slide in and about the open hatches. They find the crew and thereupon devour them. It is said they come most often when the moon is full and rises overhead."

Religious leaders were not silent on the subject either. According to a Danish bishop, Erik Pontoppidan, most seamen concluded that sea monsters stemmed from the Great Deceiver, the devil himself. In one of his books, entitled *The Natural History of Norway*, the bishop wrote: "Thorlack Thorlackson told me that in 1720 a sea serpent had been shut up a whole week in a little inlet. When it left eight days later, the skin of a great serpent was found."

In 1780 a Moslem in the port of Chanak, a city in what is now called Turkey, wrote, "By the beard of the prophet. It has struck again. Oran Karamanoglu was mending his nets by light of a great fire. Out of the waves came a form so horrible it is beyond description. Mustafa,

This drawing was used in a book called Natural History of Norway, *written by Erik Pontoppidan, Bishop of Bergen. It was published in 1752 and again in 1753. In his book, Pontoppidan wrote at length about a sea serpent called Soe Orm. This artwork was to show that at one time fishermen fired at the head of Soe Orm.* PHOTOGRAPH COURTESY OF THE FORBES COLLECTION, HART NAUTICAL MUSEUM, MASSACHUSETTS INSTITUTE OF TECHNOLOGY.

youngest son of Karamanoglu, ran for help. Upon returning, Oran was gone. Mustafa, only of years that can be counted on the fingers of two hands, said that the beast crawled on many legs, had blazing eyes and a great mouth, and roared with noises like those out of a thunderous sky. In size, he declares the animal to have been as big as a *sambuk* [a large fishing boat]."

In the late 1700s a young girl tending a lighthouse near the coastal city of Jijelli, in what is now called Algeria, reported the following: "There was a great roar that cometh out of the darkness of the sea. On looking into the blackness, eyes, many eyes, were reflected by the flames atop the tower [lighthouse]. The eyes drew close. Squealing, bawling, and making such noises, certain of the beasts crawled forward on fat bellies. I ran to get M.

49

SEA MONSTERS

Fekhikheri, my master. Upon our return, the beasts were gone. Only their tracks remained. Fekhikheri said I lied and beat me with the switch of a camel, but I know of what I had seen."

One of the most unusual reports of sea monsters at this time came out of the Far East in the late 1700s. Trade was expanding rapidly as fast sailing ships were perfected. A large Japanese junk found its way into Irish waters. It was loaded with a mixed cargo and a good many sea stories. Most Irishmen had never seen an Oriental nor the unusual ship these men sailed. So the occasion created a considerable amount of national attention.

To make the ship's arrival more startling, there was aboard an Irish missionary who was returning to the "old sod" after more than twenty years in the Far East.

The Irish found an admirable character in the shipmaster and an excellent interpreter in the priest. "The ship's master was from Yedo (now called Tokyo) and his name was Tokugawa," wrote a man named Patrick O'Malley. "His ship, while compared to most of our barques was small, carried a shipment of hair oil (made from camellia seeds), rice, sweet potatoes, tea, silk, pearls, pottery of great beauty, and saki wine. This Tokugawa spoke of a long passage in which his vessel (he called it a sampan) had been attacked by a school of fierce *ningyo*, or mermaids. They had women's bodies of a lusty build, but in place of legs had fish tails. They were led by a number of big *kappa* (men that resemble sea monsters). The crew of the sampan had beaten off the attackers with swords. Tokugawa had proof of his story. He called upon a crewman, Yoriije, who offered the dried claws of *kappa* for sale. Another of the crew, named Tsutomu, offered the dried fish tails of the *ningyo* for sale. Of all the cargo, the *ningyo* tails and the saki brought the highest price at public auction."

Apparently, throughout all the selling and telling of

stories, the clergyman offered no objection to either what was said or what was sold.

Reports of sea monsters came from the young American nation as well. In 1780, the *American Journal of Science and Arts* published an interesting letter written by a Captain George Little. "I was lying in Round Pond, in Broad Bay [known to have been somewhere between Penobscot and Portland, Maine], in a public armed ship. At sunrise, I discovered a large serpent, or sea monster, coming down the bay. It was on the surface of the water. The cutter was manned and armed. I went myself in the boat. We proceeded after the serpent. When within a hundred feet, the mariners were ordered to fire on him. Before they could make ready, the serpent dove."

Captain Little then described the monster as being from 45 to 50 feet in length. The diameter of his body was about 15 inches. His head, which he carried 4 or 5 feet out

Captain Little reported seeing his sea monster in American waters during 1780. However, as early as 1639 this sea serpent was reported to be off our New England shores. This artwork is supposed to be the earliest drawing made of a sea monster in this country. It is said to have been made at the time of the sighting. PHOTOGRAPH COURTESY OF THE FORBES COLLECTION, HART NAUTICAL MUSEUM, MASSACHUSETTS INSTITUTE OF TECHNOLOGY.

of the water, was nearly as large as that of a man. He gave the appearance of a large black snake.

The most interesting part of Little's story is the fact that he wrote it out and took a public oath as to its truth.

Shortly after Captain Little's story appeared, another showed up. The American magazine *Zoologist* printed an excerpt from the log of a ship named *General Coole.* "A very large snake passed the ship. It appeared to be 16 or 18 feet in length. It was 3 or 4 feet in circumference. The back was of light color and the belly yellow." The ship's log was signed "S. H. Saxby, Master Mariner, Bouchurch, Isle of Wight." This entry in a ship's log makes it especially noteworthy. To enter any false statement in a ship's log was then, and is now, a criminal offense. So serious was a false entry considered in the late 1700s that a certain captain was hanged from a yardarm for entering an untruth in a log.

6

. . . And More Recent Reports

T HE nineteenth century marked a period of great progress in the maritime industry. Navigators were able to find their way around the globe with pinpoint accuracy. Shipwrights (men skilled in building ships) gave thought to swifter hulls. Ships were constructed to be sturdier throughout. Ship design, drawing of plans, fastening, planking, caulking, deck laying, hewing, and a hundred other maritime skills each became an art. More and finer ships slid down the ways.

And as more ships took to the seas, more sea monster sightings were recorded. The first such report of the new century is found in the log of a Dutch pinnace named *Brinklaan* 3. A pinnace was then a heavy-planked, square-stern sailing ship. She could carry a large amount of cargo for great distances. A pinnace was a money-maker, and the thrifty Dutch loved them. The captain of this vessel, J. Haven van Vlissinger, noted that upon the stroke of eight bells (midnight), on the first day of 1800, the ship ran upon something while in open seas. "Man on watch, Wijnne Doorsen, said this was big fish. Had eyes.

Horse's head. Large teeth. Horns and skin like bullfrog. Sunrise was 0611. No damage noted. Horizon clear. Wind moderate out of north eastern quadrant."

Ships flying the American flag were becoming common sights on the oceans of the world. And reports of sea monsters along the eastern coast of the young nation were cropping up. By 1805, many Yankee logbooks were noting either sea monsters or sea serpents. A characteristic of shipmasters was the brevity of their entries in logbooks. They were neither scholars nor long-winded. The captain of the ketch *Mattapek* jotted down, "Ran afoul of a monster. Not whale. Something else." His name cannot be read, for it is too much of a scribble.

However, a Captain Parks, master of the barkentine *Four Winds*, wrote clearly, on September 18, 1807, that "Seaman Foster, whilst up fore topmast clearing topsail yard hoist, did cry out a sighting. From two points abaft the port beam appeared a serpent. Mr. Range, the bos'n was on deck. He reckoned the beast to be a mile distant and thrice the length of our largest surf boat."

Meanwhile, reports of sea monsters in European waters appeared in letters, logs, and newspaper accounts. One sea monster even became so well known that the beast was named "the animal of Stronsa," so named because its carcass was found among the rocks off the island of Stronsa, in the Hebrides. And as such it was seen in many places and written about at great length. Then came a sad day. The dead animal was washed ashore. According to a scientific journal of 1808, "The body measured 55 feet in length. The thickest part might be equal to the girth of an Orkney pony. The head was not larger than that of a seal. It was furnished with two blow holes. On each side of the body were three large fins, shaped like paws."

Dead sea monsters did not excite scientific investigations during these times. They were simply a matter of curiosity. Local interest caused them to be noted in the public press; after that they were forgotten. At sea, however, a strange animal continued as a thing to be feared. As a result, we find more attention being given to reports turned in by ship's officers. Not many deck hands could write, let alone sign their names. And many officers were not even literate. They could spell only a small number of words. An exception to this was the owner of a shipping agency in an African port called El-Sayed. This man's name was Hassan Aboud. He wrote that during the Moslem holy period of Ramadan in 1808 he had been aboard an Australian three-masted bark when it had been attacked by a sea monster. "In middle of night, with full moon on high, all aboard aroused by cry of lookout. Thinking ship to be foundering, passengers hurried on deck. There we found a horrible scene going on. Something of a hairy nature had climbed across bow and bitten, or chewed, one of the hands. By light of moon, its eyes could be seen, large as a warrior's shield. It had tusks like those of a full-grown elephant. When attacked by an ax, it uttered no sound, gave no ground, and bled but little.

"The captain, seeing a losing battle and fearing for his ship, went below. He returned with two muskets and a brace of pistols. These he fired into the animal's eyes. The monster returned to the sea.

"By light of day, it was discovered that the outer bobstay and part of bowsprit had been torn loose. On deck, a windlass had been ripped free of its base. Whilst the drumhead on the capstan was torn loose, with its barrel split through the middle. None could say of what this beast was."

Sea monster sightings were no longer isolated instances, because ships were becoming more numerous, faster, and able to travel farther. Often an animal seen in English waters would be spotted a few days later off the coast of France. Then after several weeks it would turn up in the North Sea. In other words, sightings, when plotted on a chart, showed one monster making several different appearances. Descriptions were not all alike in detail. Differences might have been due to the circumstances surrounding the person involved.

For instance, in a report made under oath at Kirkwall, Scotland, November 19, 1808, John Peace stated that he had first sighted a large dead animal while at sea. Later, he said that the monster was washed ashore. He then carefully measured it to be about "fifty-four or fifty-five feet in length." Some days later a ship's master brought his vessel to port at nearby Dunnet Bay and told of having rammed a "great beast at sea." Apparently the incident had taken place one week prior to the find made by John Peace. In the captain's case, the animal was described as "not less than two hundred feet from one end to that of the other." It is likely that the dead animal found by John Peace was the one rammed by this ship.

Another example of one marine oddity being sighted several different times is found in a series of reports dated 1809. "A serpent," reported the master of a Greek fishing boat from Mykonos, "fouled our nets. It was round of body, stout as a good-sized tree, and of twice the length of our tallest mast." One month and two days later, a Spanish felucca [a large fishing boat] came into a nearby port and told of being attacked by a beast with arms as thick as "trees in the forest." Eight weeks later a French *chasse-marée* (fishing boat) briefly reported seeing a sea monster, and two weeks after that, a German North Sea ketch complained of having its nets "torn asunder from an animal of size."

Two months after all these reports, a Portuguese barkentine came ashore to display a "remarkable beast out of the ocean." José Rodrigues Pinto, a fish merchant of Lisbon, made this statement to the press: "Capitão Fernandos da Silva Nuñes sold his entire catch at better than market price because of a most queer fish hanging from yardarm." Unfortunately, no description was given of this most queer fish.

SEA SERPENT

Engraved from a drawing taken from life as appeared in GLOUCESTER HARBOUR August 23 1817.
Boston Published by E.J. Lane and J. Row

While Europe was seeing this beast in the late 1700s, it suddenly appeared in American waters in the early 1800s. The caption at the bottom of the engraving assures us that it is "taken from life as appeared in Gloucester Harbour, August 23, 1817." PHOTOGRAPH COURTESY OF THE NAVAL HISTORICAL FOUNDATION, WASHINGTON, D.C.

It appears that the sea beast encountered first by the Greek fisherman, then by the Spanish, French, German, and Portuguese, was the same monster. Any difference in description of the animal was probably due to the size of the fishing boat. A 20-foot sea serpent would appear horribly big if seen from a rowboat, while the same animal, if noted from the deck of a three-masted deep-water vessel, would be of no alarm.

Excitement too can distort what a person sees. During the early nineteenth century a Scotsman named Donald MacLain claimed he was chased ashore by a sea monster. He ran his boat aground and scrambled to a

57

high point. Later, he wrote a report that said "it was close to eighty feet of length."

A farmer from a nearby cottage said the animal was no more than twice again as long as "my old dobbin." So we have the word of a fisherman against that of a farmer. It is hard to know who saw the sea monster with the most accuracy.

A similar disagreement is found in the reports of a sea monster off the coast of Massachusetts, in the harbor of Cape Ann, north of Gloucester. Matthew Gaffney, the mate of the brig *Cox Neck*, reported sighting a monster. He took a public oath that on August 14, 1817, he had seen a strange animal resembling a sea serpent. He got within 30 feet of the animal, and, he stated, its head was as big as a four-gallon keg and its body 40 feet long.

"Not so," claimed a fisherman named Canor. "It were twice that length." Canor said it was the same serpent he had seen an hour or two later. However, he refused to take an oath on the truth of his statement. He claimed that to do so would be against his religious principles.

At about this time, somewhere close to 1820, a woman in Philadelphia displayed a letter she had received from her brother in Bristol, Rhode Island. He wrote, "Death, dear Elizabeth, hath taken away your niece. The girl, while at a beach this summer a making of sand castles, was killed by a horrible monster what comes out of the sea. It had teeth, which it chewed upon her with. It had flappers like would be found upon a seal. Roared like a lion. Beat off four would-be rescuers. Mr. Swampscott (or maybe that is where he is from) who is keep of the beach said it was horrible. He had never before seen the likes."

Sea monsters seemed to vary like styles in wearing apparel. At times the monsters seen would all have a horse's head. Other times they would have pointed features like those of a snake. For several years they were reported as having hair. Again, for a number of

On October 18, 1848, the English gunboat Daedalus *arrived in her home port of Plymouth. Her crew told of a strange creature they had seen in the South Atlantic. Based on what was said, this drawing was made by an artist from the London* Times. *Captain M'Quhae, the shipmaster, said the animal's head appeared to be about 4 feet out of the water and there was close to 60 feet of body in a straight line. He calculated another 30 to 40 feet was underwater.* PHOTOGRAPH COURTESY OF GEORGE M. CUSHING.

years, they had bodies smooth and scaleless. This trend is somewhat frustrating. Were people seeing the same beast? Or were they suffering from group hysteria? It is hard to believe that so many people, in such distant places, were suffering the same delusions.

As an example of this, there was the case of a

sighting made aboard the sailing ship *Sacramento*. She
was out of New York, captained by William H. Nelson,
and of "square rigged standing." On reaching Melbourne,
Australia, he reported that he personally had observed a
monster while at sea. "Thick about as a whisky barrel, of
brownish color, it had a flat head."

Two weeks later, the four-masted bark *Swordfish*,
captained by a Briton known only as Hetherington, put
in at Honolulu. The captain reported having sighted a sea
serpent while under way. "I myself mounted to the
maintop crosstree. From that vantage point a beast was
observed. It was just two points off the starboard bow. It
was of a brownish color, flat of features and possessed
coils as large around as the base of our own lower mast."

There is a great deal of similarity between these two
reports. Yet it is hardly likely that either captain ever
heard of the other. Certainly, it was unlikely they would
suffer the same hallucination. Each was a knowledgeable
seaman. Each was certain of what he had observed. And
what they saw was very likely the same beast.

Toward the end of the 1800s, reports of sea monster
sightings in the Indian Ocean came to light. The British
had occupied India and their ships controlled the Arabian
Sea, much of the Indian Ocean, and the Bay of Bengal. As
a consequence, commerce and passenger service were
common throughout this portion of the world. Letters to
England told of sea monsters, military reports included
accounts of maneuvers involving the monsters, and jour-
nalists recorded all the excitement. Typical of these
reports is the abrupt account by a British regimental
sergeant-major taking a detail of troops from Madras to
a post at Bhubaneswar.

"Two days out. Seas calm. Numerous troops sick.
Just a lot of rot. Altogether mental. Ship steady as your
Aunt Betsy's kitchen floor. Standing on after deck
enjoying breeze at high noon. One of lower ratings,
named Medways, alongside chattering about his cottage
in Sussex. Suddenly he pointed. A bit off the end of the

vessel was a black object. Long, I should say. About fifty feet. Maybe more. The bloody thing seemed alive. By jove, it was. Sort of swimming like. Not quite a snake. Had sort of loops, or humps that moved up and down. 'Here you,' I says to one of me men. 'Leg it to the ship's captain and draw his attention to this beast.' Off he goes. But I hear no more about it from that quarter. The captain's a bit of a snob. After a time, this thing, or whatever it was, slid under the surface."

Perhaps the most unusual sea monster report of this period is to be found in the library of the Naval Museum at Greenwich, England. A deck rating on a military ship was court-martialed on the charge that he had "given call to a false report while standing his watch at sea." As the trial progressed, it turned into a scientific inquiry. Several other enlisted men aboard swore that they, too, had seen the beast. Unfortunately, none of the officers had. The accused, so the charge read, had simply given the alarm to relieve the monotony of his watch. In the questioning of the sailor, the following dialogue took place:

Q. You say it was near the end of your watch?
A. Aye, your honor, not quite six bells.
Q. There was sufficient light by which you could see?
A. The sun was just a nubbin over the horizon.
Q. Tell us what you saw.
A. A thing what had one devilish big hump to its back. There was a neck too. A long one, topped off by a horse's head.
Q. And how long was the entire animal?
A. From what I could see of it, m'lord, a little under half a cable [300 feet].
Q. And you called an alarm?
A. No, sir. I rung the ship's bell a number of rapid strokes to indicate danger. There ain't no call what I knows of for sighting a sea monster.

SEA MONSTERS

Another seaman on watch confirmed the accused man's sighting. He, however, saw the animal a little differently. "This here beast—he weren't no fish—had a long neck topped off by a chicken's head. Had a beak to its snout, it did, and big eyes."

Q.   And how long would you say it was?
A.   About the length of our main lower topsail yard [close to 100 feet].

A scientist was finally called in. He agreed that such a sea beast might exist. He readily admitted that little was known about the deepest waters of the sea. So the accused sailor was discharged by the court as being "truthful in the dispatch of his duties."

The late 1800s saw many changes in ships and shipbuilding. Steam power was rapidly replacing the sail. In 1881 the *Servia*, a merchant vessel capable of crossing the ocean in seven days from London to New York, was the first ship to be made of steel. Seven years after that came the famous *Philadelphia*. She was the first twin-screw ship ever launched. Soon steamships were traveling to remote areas, and geographic discoveries were being made almost daily. Scientists were able to travel farther afield at a faster pace.

Now sea monster reports were heard from the remote corners of the world. The news media carried stories of huge serpents, hairy water beasts, and great animals out of the depths. The beasts were no longer considered entirely fictitious, and at last came to the attention of scientists as well as sea captains.

Although sea monsters were spotted frequently in European waters, during the early 1900s public attention centered on America. American sightings were better authenticated. The beasts involved were bigger, they stayed in one neighborhood longer, and above all, they were seen by a greater variety of people.

Typical of these years was the sea monster sighted

from the yacht *Valhalla,* in the Atlantic, somewhere south of Florida. Although a privately owned vessel, she was on a voyage of oceanographic research. She was 1,700 tons and capable of steaming at about 11 knots (11 nautical miles per hour). Her owner, Lord Lindsay, Earl of Crawford, a prominent astronomer, was taking her on an extended cruise through American waters. He had aboard his friends E. G. B. Meade-Waldo and M. J. Nicoll, both prominent scientists of the early 1900s. All three men were respected members of the British Zoological Society.

On December 7, 1905, at 10:15 A.M. an object surfaced about 100 yards from the yacht. Mr. Meade-Waldo de-

The Valhalla *sea monster was sighted on December 7, 1905, at 10:15 A.M. The name of the beast is taken from the yacht shown in the background. Although the vessel was on a scientific cruise in warm waters south of Florida, its exact location at the time of the sighting is not known. One of the scientists aboard received an indication of position from the captain but wrote, "I think this is not correct." However, it has been accepted that the animal was somewhere south of Key West.* PHOTOGRAPH COURTESY OF ILLUSTRATED LONDON NEWS.

63

scribed it in these words: "I saw a large fin, or frill, sticking out of the water. It was dark seaweed-brown in color, somewhat crinkled at the edge. It was apparently about six feet in length and projected from eighteen inches to two feet from the water."

He turned a pair of powerful German binoculars on the peculiar object that all were now watching. "A great head and neck rose out of the water in front of the frill," he later reported to the Zoological Society. "The neck appeared about the thickness of a man's body. It was from seven to eight feet out of the water. The head and neck were all of about the same thickness."

Mr. Nicoll added his view to this same report. "The head had a turtle-like appearance and had eyes. I could see the line of the mouth, but we were sailing fast and drew away from the object." However, he noted that the animal "moved its head and neck from side to side in a peculiar manner."

Later, both the first mate and the third mate who were on duty aboard the *Valhalla* saw a commotion in the water. Since the yacht was doing research work, they put about and, at 8½ knots, tried to close on the object. Although they came alongside what was apparently a large sea beast, it stayed just beneath the surface. Mr. Simmons, the first mate, wrote into the ship's log, "It was not a whale, was not blowing, and neither [he] nor the third mate had ever seen such a creature."

So well was this sighting documented that the animal became known as the "great sea serpent." However, because this account of the sea serpent came from prominent scientists, other reports were neglected. Three days after the yacht reported the occasion, the log of the merchant sailing ship *Happy Warrior* read: "A sea snake of great magnitude appeared off our port bow. Was several lengths our ship. Had long neck. Sounded after few minutes. Estimated speed six knots."

This brief report is noteworthy for several reasons.

The captain of the ship was only about 80 miles from the yacht *Valhalla* at the time. And as near as can be judged, the *Happy Warrior* was not a small ship. She was described as "three masted, full rigged ship, with skysails and main moonsail."

One week later a small brig, manned by a crew of deaf mutes, put in at Key West to replenish water supplies. Although none could talk, one man, who appeared to be their leader, scribbled off a note to a native standing nearby. "Seen serpent. Big it was. Maybe size of big tree, twice size of mainmast." All that is known of this particular sailing ship is that she flew the American flag and was either named *Ruth B.* or *Ruby*, both of which were in the same general area at about the same time.

World War I was just over the horizon. Both Germany and England were scouting out American waters for possible military use. Many of the ships were involved in sea monster sightings off American shores. Unfortunately, because of military secrecy, the sightings were recorded only in the ships' logbooks—and sometimes not even there. The reports were never made public. One example is found in the records taken from the German raider *Wolf*. This ship left Germany and sailed the seas for fourteen months. She roved along the American shores, visited the Indian Ocean, and went as far afield as Australia. The chief mate, Hans Schmidt, wrote that they had come upon a "great beast of long-necked dimensions just off the coast of New England. Not wishing to draw public attention to ourselves, we swore all hands to secrecy."

During World War I, many records of sea monster sightings were lost when merchant ships, torpedoed by German U-boats, sank and carried their log books to the ocean floor.

Probably most noteworthy of any such incident was the sinking of the British freighter H.M.S. *Hilary*.

SEA MONSTERS

Although the ship's log was lost, the crew was saved. The captain recounted that on May 22, 1917, a few days before the *Hilary* was sunk, the ship was in the North Atlantic. The weather was excellent. There was hardly a breeze and the surface of the water was calm. He was in his cabin, directly beneath the bridge, doing some paper work. The officer on watch called down, "Cap'n, object on starboard quarter."

The captain came to the bridge at a run. He was fearful that it was a German submarine. "Is it a periscope?" he asked.

"No," the officer of the watch answered. "It looks more like a living thing. But it is not a whale."

The captain grabbed his binoculars and had a long look. Whatever it was, it had a dorsal fin and a peculiar head. Since the ship's gun crew were in need of target practice, he told his lieutenant commander to sound the ship's alarm. Like most armed merchant ships, the vessel had two six-pounders (guns that use six-pound shells) mounted just behind the bridge.

Out of curiosity, the captain decided to put his ship about and have a closer look at the animal. "We passed it about thirty yards off our starboard side. We got a very good look," he said.

"The head was about the shape of a cow, through which horns were sticking. It was black, except for the front of the face. This could clearly be seen to have a stripe of whitish flesh between its nostrils. As we passed, the head raised itself two or three times, apparently to get a good look at the ship."

The captain was anxious to verify what was before him, so he asked several others how long they thought the neck of the animal to be.

A young lieutenant answered, "The length of one of our lifeboats [28 feet]."

"Not less than fifteen feet," another said.

The captain himself thought the neck to be about 20

feet long. Assuming the dorsal fin to be just behind the junction of neck and body, he guessed the entire body to be about 60 feet long. Unfortunately for the *Hilary*, at 7 A.M. several days later, a U-boat torpedoed the ship and it sank.

Several years later, as documents, which included logbooks, naval yard relics, and official correspondence, were slowly drifting into the British Museum, a letter was received from a Commander Youngblood of the Royal Navy. He wrote that as the officer in charge of a "kill-class gunboat" (a small vessel used during World War I to pursue German U-Boats) on patrol, he had observed a peculiar animal in the sea. "According to my personal log, it was on 15 April 1917. We were in the North Atlantic on station." The letter goes on to say that on a calm day, the alarm was sounded. It was believed that the periscope of a German U-boat was seen. On steaming down on the object, it suddenly became obvious that they were closing in on a peculiar animal. "It had a long neck, a head somewhat like that of a horse and a big dorsal fin."

According to Commander Youngblood, the beast showed no fear of the warship. It raised a long neck and took a good look. "We were about to get closer," he wrote, "when a wireless message was received saying a nearby ship was under submarine attack. We left the scene at flank speed."

Was this the same beast spotted by the *Hilary*? No one will ever know for sure. However, it is logical to assume that it was. Both ships were in the same general area. Each had a good look at the monster. And above all, descriptions tallied.

During these times most descriptions of sea monsters were recorded by people aboard surface ships; yet the Germans had hundreds of U-boats of all sizes cruising through the oceans of the world. These submarines were of all sizes: some were large and able to travel very far, others were small and cruised only near their home base. All were well armed, dangerous, and captained by brave men. Most of these submarines were hunted down by American and British warships and sunk. Only a few of their records were saved. An Admiral von Holtzendorff, in a personal letter to an Admiral Koch, mentioned the sighting of a sea serpent. He warned that it was probably a British trick. "They might be floating decoys. By such a guise, they could lure our submarines into coming closer. Thereby getting a better shot," he wrote.

As if to disprove the belief that sea monsters were little more than a trick, the Flanders U-Boat Flotilla had an interesting experience. The UB-10 (UB for "undersea boat") turned in a report signed by a Commander Schultze. His boat was only one of thirty-six submarines belonging to this flotilla. "We were cruising at thirty feet beneath the surface of the ocean," he wrote. "We were working as a team with U-15 and U-18. Suddenly we ran headlong into something. We began to sink bow down. Blowing all tanks and giving full forward thrust, we managed to surface.

"On reaching the conning tower, we found that the bow had pierced some sort of animal. It was not a whale. It had a long neck, body like an elephant and a head resembling a very large turtle. The beast was all of fifty feet in length.

"We were operating in enemy waters and stood in danger of being attacked. Yet I could not maneuver with so much dead weight hanging from the bow. Hurriedly, I set all hands hacking at the remains. It took about four hours to clear the deck."

Later, as defeat closed in on the German fleet, the UB-85 was surprised floating on the surface. The British patrol boat *Coreopsis*, commanded by Lieutenant P. S. Peat, R.N.R., closed on the target. Firing at a rapid rate, her guns hit the submarine. The boat began to sink. The crew abandoned their stricken vessel and were picked up by several patrol boats that also closed in. One of these was the *Valororus*. She picked up the captain of the German U-boat, Lieutenant Commander Krech, who had a strange story to tell.

"Two nights before," Krech reported, "my submarine was on the surface recharging batteries. The moon was up and I was very nervous. We could easily be seen by any enemy patrol boat. Without any kind of warning, a strange beast began to climb aboard. The great weight of the animal gave us a list to starboard. We were in danger of shipping water through an open hatch and sinking.

"This beast had large eyes, set in a horny sort of skull. It had a small head, but with teeth that could be seen glistening in the moonlight. Every man on watch began firing a sidearm at the beast. It had a hold on the forward gun mount and would not turn loose. After a vicious struggle, in which my boat was almost swamped, the beast dropped back into the sea."

Unfortunately for the German U-boat, severe damage had been done to her forward deck plating. She could no longer submerge. Water would flood into the forward compartments. "That is why," the German skipper said, "you were able to catch us on the surface."

7

Three Perspectives

AS the twentieth century progressed, it became evident that there were three different angles from which sea monsters had been seen. There was the perspective of the sea captain, that of the deep-sea diver, and that of the oceanographer. Each could be viewing the same beast in very different encounters.

The captain views the sea from a ship's bridge. He is out there, in faraway seas, during all kinds of weather. He sees his domain at every turn of the clock. Most of these men are strong individuals, positive of what they have seen. Captain Burton Wilmslow was typical of such hardy souls. An Englishman who had been aboard ships since boyhood, he knew the seas of the world as a London taxi driver knows the streets of his city. Wilmslow's mother had died on his twelfth birthday, during the worst of the great Depression. His dad, who had a strong fondness for the boy, was master of a tramper named *Shun Wing*. It was a ship of 6,987 gross tons, not big as ships go. The old vessel had been sold, resold, and sold again. After her engines were all but worn out from pounding a passage from one part of the world to another, she was sold again, this time into the Koo Wong Navigation Company of Hong Kong.

"That's when my father became master," Captain Wilmslow said. "Not much of a ship, really. But in those days any berth was a good berth. Besides, the company let my dad take me along as cabin boy.

"Our run was generally from Kwangchow [Canton, China], over to Puerto Princesa [an island in the South China Sea], on southward to Ketapang [Borneo], in and out through the Indonesian Islands and back through the Philippine Sea. These were strange waters in many ways, and indeed we witnessed many strange events.

"That is when I saw my first sea monster—at age sixteen, from the decks of the *Shun Wing*, when we were steaming slowly through the Sulu Sea. It was in the evening, sometime just after three bells (5:30 P.M.). My dad had the watch and was pacing the port wing of the bridge. I had just delivered a pot of hot tea to the bridge and was close at hand. Suddenly my father stopped his pacing. 'Get me my binoculars, boy,' he said. By the time I'd picked up the glasses from the wheelhouse and returned to the port wing, I could see what he was looking at.

"Just abaft [astern] the *Shun Wing* was what looked like a string of small boats in tow of a larger boat. As I watched, the whole thing changed shape. Then I could see it was a serpent of some sort. Maybe forty or fifty feet long, it had a row of dorsal fins running along its back.

" 'Sound the whistle,' my dad called to the helmsman. With that we let out a mighty blast. The noise attracted the beast's attention. It turned a peculiar-looking head in our direction and stared hard. The head looked to be about like the head of a drum fish, only with ears and a neck.

" 'Port five,' my father called. I could see he intended to run the beast down. As we came around, the beast

71

adjusted its direction so that we got no closer. By then every man in the crew was lining the rails. The ship's whistle had brought them running.

"A Mr. Yang Lee was the navigator. He had a pair of binoculars on the beast. Then that thing was gone and everyone fell to arguing about what it was.

"My father entered it in the logbook. I'll never forget his words. So brief and to the point. 'Sighted sea monster. Opinion of those having binoculars was that beast seemed to be about fifty feet in length. Showed large eyes, teeth, and loops to body.' "

Another British captain had a more horrifying story to tell. In 1971, W. N. Lindsay Cosby-Philipps was master of the freighter *King George* of the China Line, Ltd., members of the British Commonwealth Shipping Group. The ship weighed 8,331 gross tons and had oil engines that could turn up 13 knots. "We were making that long haul, of about 5,000 miles, from the Samoa Islands northwest to the Philippines, when the man standing watch on the fo'c'sle head gave a cry. Then he rang the ship's bell. It was too late. We hit something a solid lick.

"At the time, it was my watch below. But I made the bridge in a hurry. The chief mate had the duty and had already rung for STOP on the engine room telegraph. But in that type vessel it would take fifteen or twenty minutes to come to a stop. So we kept on going at a fast clip.

" 'An animal,' the chief called, 'we hit some sort of animal. Maybe it was a whale.'

"Then, off to starboard, a sizable head came out of the ocean. It was followed by a neck. This neck appeared to be attached to a big lump of a body. The thought went through my mind that it was a hippopotamus that had been washed out to sea. Then I could see it had a long tail. Not quite a fish tail, more like a snake's tail that had been flattened out a bit at the end.

"This beast had an enormous mouth, which it opened wide. The mouth showed two tusks on the lower jaw. It

72

uttered no cry, but turned and butted us in the forward part. That was a solid smash. It vibrated through the entire ship. We were still moving ahead at perhaps 8 knots, but the beast had no trouble staying alongside. Every once in a while it would crash against our starboard bow. We were taking a beating. By now, I had a man on the bridge firing a heavy-caliber rifle into the animal. After about six shots, it sank slowly out of sight."

Unfortunately, the *King George* started taking on water in the forward hold. Because of this, when the ship finally limped into Tandag harbor, in the Philippines, there was an inquiry. The ship needed some costly repairs. It was thought that the captain was covering up a collision at sea. However, the chief mate took a lie-detector test after giving the following testimony under oath:

"Whenever the beast would surface, it generally spouted a column of air from either nostril, snorting loudly as it did so. It had small eyes near the top of its head, tiny ears, a neck maybe ten or twelve feet long, and a body that showed no scales."

"Could it have been some sort of land animal that got washed out to sea?" he was asked.

"Hardly likely. It was too handy in the water and had a tail like that of a fish," he answered.

One of the strangest, and probably best documented, sea monster stories to be found anywhere is recorded in the Colonial Secretary's File of the Archives, State Library, Melbourne, Australia. Written testimony submitted by the officer of the watch and others tells clearly what happened to the steamer *Kuranda*.

"During January 1973," the officer on watch testified, "I joined the Australian Steam Navigation Company, Ltd. I was second officer on the 1,483-ton vessel *Kuranda* under command of Captain Langley Smith. We sailed out of Sydney, destined for Viti Levu in the Fiji Islands. After two days at sea we ran into heavy seas rolling in from the north-northeast. Our bow was driving directly into the seas. It soon became apparent that the ship had been improperly loaded. She showed herself to be heavy in the forward hold. Because of this, the vessel took on a deep pitch. She would bury her head into an oncoming sea, go far under, then slowly rise to spray sea water into the wind. The old man [captain] tried altering course to ease the pitch. Something heavy in number-one hold broke loose and set up a smashing fit to split our seams. We had to turn back into the seas. That eased the thumping a bit, but renewed the sickening pitch.

"At shortly after eight bells in the midday watch, at which time I was officer of the deck, the ship took an especially deep pitch. Water buried the entire forward part of the ship. It went clear out of sight. It seemed to me as if the ship might run herself under. Although I can't be sure, it seemed to me that at this moment there was sort of a bump up forward. It was as if we had hit something. The ship seemed slow to make a recovery. Her head stayed down for what seemed unusually long. So at 12:32 I thumped my heel three times on the deck over the captain's cabin. That was a signal something was wrong. He came arunning. Right away he sensed that things were not just right. It appeared as though our bow had scooped something out of the sea.

"When I got a look at what was hanging on the bows, one devil of a shock ran through me. Draped over the entire fo'c'sle head was a monstrous glob that resembled a gigantic jellyfish. It must have weighed twenty tons. It had tentacles that swirled back across the deck, enveloping the wheelhouse and each wing of the bridge. The seaman on lookout, fellow named McGiniss, had been stationed on the port wing. Some of this tentacle stuff got wrapped around him. He fell to the deck screaming. The captain and I managed to drag him into the wheelhouse. He looked as if he'd been scalded by live steam. Wherever those tentacles had touched, they had burned him.

"We were now dangerously low by the head. So much

extra weight threatened to run the ship under. Our screw [propeller] was half out of the water. We had little or no forward thrust. The bosun came running. He said number-one hold was shipping water at a fast rate. The captain put out an SOS. Luckily, the deep-sea salvage tug *Hercules* was within 500 miles of our position. That's a twenty-four-hour steam even for a fast ship. But *Hercules* was new and her captain said she could make it in less than that.

"Meantime, the old man tried every trick in the book to get rid of that poisonous beast skewered on our bow. There was no way he could shake it off. The tentacles were dangerous. They had stingers that could poison a man to death in minutes. The deck was two feet deep with this jelly-like mass. McGiniss, the seaman on watch that had been struck by tentacles, was now dead.

"We dared not go out on deck to try and shovel the thing loose. With every wave we took aboard, those slimy arms swirled all around the ship. It is my estimate that some of them were no less than two hundred feet long."

The captain of the deep-sea rescue vessel *Hercules* gave his testimony: "At two minutes past three bells [1:32 P.M.] we received a wireless signal from S.S. *Kuranda* saying she needed help. I put about and proceeded in their direction. On arrival, I found the ship enveloped by a giant box jellyfish. The bellows part was hung onto the ship's bow. The tentacles lay back along the entire length of the ship. We manned two high-pressure hoses, using live steam, and after two hours we managed to get most of that animal washed loose. It was dangerous work. The seas were running heavy and it was risky closing in on the ship. Finally the weather abated a bit and we got two auxiliary pumps aboard the *Kuranda*. That lowered the forward hold level of water. We accompanied the ship back to Sydney."

A later analysis of remains found aboard the freighter proved the monster taken aboard the bow of the *Kuranda* was a giant species of a lion's-mane jellyfish, which is sometimes called a wasp, hairy stinger, or great sea nettle.

Perhaps those aboard *Kuranda* were luckier than they realized. For the *Times* of London carried a story somewhat similar. Unfortunately, it ended in absolute horror. In 1874 the steamer *Strathowen*, bound for Madras, from Colombo, sighted a sailing ship on a placid sea. As people aboard the steamer watched, a dark object rose out of the water. It was a gigantic beast of some sort. It moved over to the ship, climbed aboard, and turned it on its side. The vessel sank within minutes.

The captain of the ship, James Floyd, was one of the few saved. The name of the vessel was the *Pearl*. He, like so many other captains before him, took an oath as to what had happened. In this case, the master's testimony was verified by those aboard the *Strathowen*.

Deep-sea divers have had many strange experiences while underwater. Unfortunately, few if any of these men are of the literary type, and they seldom write of what they have experienced. When they do, it is in a jargon hard to understand. However, they seem to like to talk. Get a group of "compressed-air workers"—as they call themselves—sitting around between dives and you hear strange stories. They relate all kinds of horrors that have befallen them while below the surface of the sea. Somehow, they thwarted death by staying cool, by using their heads, by never panicking.

Buck Johnson, an early deep-sea diver of considerable fame, described the quiet undersea world: "You reach a level where there are certain kinds of fish, snakes, and unknown sea life. You learn to master such an environment. Then you have to go deeper. It gets darker. Suddenly you find yourself having to deal with a new type of beast that no one has ever seen before. So every time you change depths, you find some new sort of monster waiting to give you a battle."

Not every diver can stand the strain. In 1970 an apprentice diver named John Williams was lowered to a great depth in the Ionian Sea off the shores of Greece. After a short while he signaled frantically to be pulled to the surface. When he was hauled aboard and his helmet removed, he announced, "I quit."

It was several hours before they could get Williams to tell his story. "My descent was alongside a cliff. It went straight down. At the bottom lay the wreck we were after. There was a hole in her side big enough to drive a bloody lorry through. This was where the gold was. So I walks in, dragging my pipe and line with me. Something warned me to stop. It was sort of an instinctive feeling that I was in the presence of some sort of an enemy.

"Then I looks straight ahead. My heart came near to stopping. A large pair of eyes were watching me. These eyes were each maybe twelve inches big. They seemed to be full of hate and anger. As I watched, the lids were raised and lowered, curtain-like, half over the eyes. I felt myself being hypnotized by the force of those big eyes. Then the eyes moved, as though the beast were coming closer. That broke the spell. I backed out and surfaced."

Another deep-sea diver, as he probed into the depths of the Baltic Sea in 1971, found the sunken ocean liner he was looking for. It was at a depth that allowed little or no sunlight to penetrate. By sense of touch, he found his way to the purser's office. There, he knew, the gold was hidden inside a big safe. As he inched along a narrow passageway, he touched something alive. He put out a hand. It came in contact with round, firm flesh. The flesh felt human. It had no scales and there was a certain warmth about it. However, the ship had been on the bottom for over a year. No human being could still be alive. Carefully, he tried to get around whatever it was that blocked his passage. It was too big. Half in anger at finding this unknown thing between him and $4 million in gold, he raised a lead-booted foot and kicked. There was a smash, a rush, and something knocked the diver flat. "It was as if a freight train ran over me," said diver Barney Burwood. "Then this thing fouled my lines, snatched me out of the passageway, whipped me clear of the ship, and banged me to the floor of the ocean."

That was enough for one day. Burwood signaled to be pulled topside. However, he had been at a great depth. In order not to develop a sickness called "the bends," he had to be raised slowly. It was over an hour before he was hauled aboard the tender. There he found himself the center of great excitement. Everyone was talking at once. They all wanted to know what he had seen. Then he explained that it was so dark he had seen nothing. This appeared to disappoint them. Then the truth came out. "A mighty big sea monster of some sort shot to the surface," the captain explained. "This brute had a head that looked like something with a pig's snout, was sort of formed like a snake, and was fringed with either hair or seaweed."

"What worried us," the captain explained, "was the fact it kept circling around for thirty or more minutes. We fired a few rifle shots at it and after a bit it disappeared. There was no knowing if it had gone back after you, or what."

A young diver named Hans Holzer told of a somewhat similar experience in the Bay of Bengal in 1972. "It was with a monstrous sea animal I'd never seen before. A real beast. It had the face and head of what looked like a wart hog. It just had to be the ugliest animal in the world. Anyhow, I'm down under, cutting an opening into the vault of a sunken passenger liner, when the bulkhead gave way and crashed in on me."

Apparently the crash stunned him for a few moments. When he regained his senses, it was pitch black inside the ship. After feeling around, he regained his underwater cutting torch. It was fitted with an automatic spark lighting system. This permitted the diver to light his flame under water. "That's when I saw this beast. It was caught between two plates of steel that had shifted. These plates held it tight. Just as if it were caught in a vise."

From Holzer's description, the undersea animal had a massive head that tapered into a long snout. At the end of the snout were two upthrust tusks. At the top of the head were a pair of piglike eyes and small horns. "There was about ten feet of that animal showing," he said, "and every inch was pure fury. It was rip-snorting mad at being hung up and tried to snap at me and my torch."

Then, in terror, Holzer also realized that the beast was between him and the companionway through which he had entered. Whenever he would start inching toward the door, the monster would lunge at him.

"The only thing to do was to give him a taste of that lighted torch," he recalled. "This I had to do carefully. If that beast ever managed to knock the cutter out of my hand, it would automatically shut off. In the dark, I'd be like a bowl of porridge in that monster's jaws. So the two of us entered into a fencing match. I'd inch toward the opening. That ugly beast would lunge. I'd poke my flame at it. Then I'd inch forward a couple of more yards. Once or twice that serpent, or whatever it was, got a taste of my torch. That made it a little more cautious. Finally, after what seemed like hours, but was really only minutes, I made my escape."

When Holzer reached the deck of the tender, some of the men wanted to go down and hook the beast. They recognized that it would be a rare and valuable find. The captain had other ideas. There was almost $2 million in gold bars within that vault and the weather was turning nasty. "We're here to bring up gold, not a sea monster," he said. With that he sent an underwater demolition specialist down with explosives.

"One bang," said Holzer, "and there wasn't enough of that beast left to stuff a sausage."

Divers generally agree that recovering human bodies

is the most distasteful job of any undersea work. It doesn't take long before all kinds of marine animals swarm around to chew on the remains. Pappy Gewinn, an old hand at such a task, had to go inside a sunken German U-boat in the Scottish Sea during the spring of 1940. His task was to bring up members of the crew who had drowned inside the submarine.

"The conning tower hatch was open, so I had no trouble getting inside," he said. "My electric flashlight lit up the interior. Suddenly I was being welcomed aboard by the dead captain. He came toward me, arms extended as though in greeting, eyes wide open and his uniform in perfect order, even to a neatly perched cap.

"It took me several moments before I realized that his heavy knee boots were loaded with water and acted like lead ballast. They kept him floating in an upright position."

Unfortunately, when Gewinn tried to go through a lower hatch, his way was blocked by the "biggest sea serpent [he'd] ever seen." "It had a head like a bulldog and mean-looking eyes," he said. "From what I could see of it, there were gills behind the head and maybe about twenty feet of flat body beyond that. While the dead submarine commander seemed to watch, I slammed the lower hatch closed and dogged it tight. Then I took my dead friend through the conning tower hatch, closed it after us, and got to the surface as fast as I could.

"When I told them about the sea serpent, it was decided to let the dead crew remain where they were until the boat was raised and the bodies could be recovered without fear of the serpent."

One of the best-known and most hunted sea monsters is the huge creature that is said to inhabit the Scottish lake Loch Ness. As early as A.D. 565, the Irish missionary Saint Columba reported seeing a huge monster rise out of the water and swim in the early-morning

The Loch Ness monster as seen by Dr. R. K. Wilson, a London surgeon, during the summer of 1934. There was mist on the water when he saw "Nessie." The camera he took the picture with had a 12-inch lens. After the incident, the doctor said he guessed the animal had a neck about 6 feet long. At the time of the sighting, he was standing on the shore near Urquhart Castle. This area seems to be one of "Nessie's" favorite feeding grounds. PHOTOGRAPH COURTESY OF LOCH NESS PHENOMENA INVESTIGATION BUREAU.

mist. Fifteen hundred years later, in 1975, Father Gregory Brusey, a priest living along the shores of this lake, pointed to where he, too, had seen a monster. "It was a long-necked animal," he said. "It was very large in size, and swam with great speed."

Between these two sightings, many hundreds of other people have come forward to say that they have seen a giant beast swimming in Loch Ness. Schoolteachers, doctors, policemen, judges, athletes, firemen, and even oceanographers have reported seeing the monster. But in spite of its great size, the big beast swims too fast and dives too rapidly to be studied closely. It remains a mystery.

One of the most amazing features of this elusive beast has been its ability to thwart numerous scientific investigations. The Massachusetts Institute of Technology has sent some of its most capable scientists to track the monster down. Harvard's Museum of Comparative Zoology has tried its hand at proving, or disproving, the presence of such a beast. Even the Smithsonian Institution, in Washington, D.C., has sent oceanographers to the lake. All have failed to one degree or another. Or at least they have not been able to lay a hand on the beast. However, they do seem able to agree on one important factor: there *is* something there!

Loch Ness is in the far northern part of Scotland. This is mountainous country that is very poor for farming. Only a few people live close to the lake, for it turns terribly cold during the winter. The lake itself begins outside the city of Inverness and runs for 24 miles among the surrounding hills. It is one of the largest lakes in all of Great Britain. However, while it is not long compared to such American lakes as Superior or Michigan, it is very deep. In places the water is 970 feet in depth. One odd feature about the lake is that it is only a mile and a half wide at its widest point. It is surrounded by heavily wooded mountains that roll upward to almost 3,000 feet. Along the rivers flowing into the lake are pleasant little towns with strange names like Inchnacardoch, Glockossean, and Drumnadrochi. The people who live nearby are friendly and speak English with a Scottish accent that can hardly be understood by an outsider.

Yet for all their neighborliness, there is said to be a dark curse that hangs over the lake. There are those who claim that devil worship has long been practiced by some of the country folk, that black magic and mystic rituals are secretly conducted along the shores of Loch Ness, that murders have been committed in the black of night, and bodies found hanging in the woods or floating face down in the cold water of the lake. District leaders laugh at such stories and say, "They are false and told by mischief makers." But on a dark night when the wind howls across the lake, it is the leaders who are first to bolt their doors against the spell of a demon.

"Nessie," as local people have come to lovingly call their lake monster, was first hunted by the English government during the summer of 1934. Sir Edward Mountain, with the approval of King George V, led a twenty-man team in a watch over the waters. Their plan was to catch the monster in daylight and take a few photographs. Nessie, however, does not pose for pictures under such perfect circumstances. It appears only in the mist of early morning or in the deep shadows of the late evening. Father Brusey, in describing his sighting, said it took place at a time when the lake monster was able to duck into a fog bank. Most other people lucky enough to have seen Nessie generally agree that a good deal of mist was on the water.

Scuba divers have tried their luck at spotting the huge animal. "The trouble is," said one, "the waters of Loch Ness are black. Millions of tiny pieces of soft coal are constantly being washed into the lake. They make it impossible to see below the surface. Underwater photography is out of the question."

One American, a young scientist from Atlanta, Georgia, brought a small submarine to Loch Ness. He was able to see something on his radar screen. His tiny vessel, however, was too slow to catch up with the beast. Commercial fishing ships travel the lake, for these waters hold big catches of tasty fish. The captains of many such boats have reported spotting Nessie on their electronic fish finders.

People who have seen the monster of Loch Ness describe it in different ways. Some say it is a long-necked beast with many humps. Others agree to the long neck but say the animal showed no humps. Still others say both descriptions are wrong. Nessie is rounded, much like a whale, and shows no neck or head. All do agree on one point: Nessie moves fast. Further, most believe that the monster is very shy. Once it is spotted, it dives out of sight.

Professor Colin Magregor, of the University of Scotland, has found a possible answer. He has spent years in studying motion pictures, radar imprints, still photographs, and written reports of Nessie. "This monster does exist," he agrees. "Furthermore, it is a type of marine animal that can breathe in three ways. First, on the surface. Second, through gills while under water. And third, through its skin during long periods of hiding in mud at the bottom of the lake."

Based on his findings, the professor says, "there is only one marine animal with all three such abilities. That is a giant fresh-water eel. Such fish were once plentiful."

As an example of the type of animal he has in mind, Professor Magregor points to Uruguay. "In a deep lake, near the city of Paysandú, they found the remains of a fresh-water eel 40 feet in length," he notes.

A fish of that size would indeed be about right for Nessie. At times it could show a head, at other times only humps or both head and humps. "A giant eel," says the professor, "would fit all descriptions."

Alex Knox, one of the fishing captains, agrees. He's a rough-hewn Scotsman who has fished Loch Ness for over thirty years. "What Magregor says makes sense. The electronic fish finder on my boat has spotted an underwater animal on more than one trip through the lake. Once we were able to stay over the beast for 18 minutes. It was at a depth of 52 feet, moving at 6 miles per hour, had a length of 24 feet 6 inches, and was shaped like an eel."

Loch Ness has been made famous by Nessie. In recent years, thousands of tourists have traveled into what was once considered out-of-the-way country. Groups of scientists, such as those of the Applied Science/New York Times expedition of June, 1976, have centered world attention on this tiny body of water. A modern highway has now been built around the entire lake. During the tourist season, lines of big passenger buses carry the curious out to the lake for a quick glimpse of the monster's home waters. The local people love all this attention, since it creates business and puts money into their pockets.

Tourists are not the only ones curious about Nessie. Scientists around the world have also begun to debate the matter among themselves. Sir Peter Scott, head of the World Wildlife Fund and Chancellor of Birmingham University in England, firmly believes that the monster is alive and doing just fine. Adrien J. Desmond, a well-known scientist, has some doubts. He claims there are not

"Nessie," as seen by local people. In 1975 the author spent many weeks along the shores of Loch Ness interviewing thirty-three local people who had seen the monster. This drawing is a composite based on all their descriptions. Those interviewed were a judge, a bus driver, doctors, barristers, traffic wardens, and other Scottish people of good reputation.

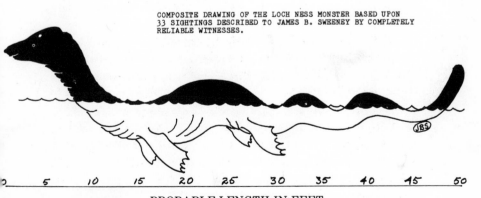

COMPOSITE DRAWING OF THE LOCH NESS MONSTER BASED UPON 33 SIGHTINGS DESCRIBED TO JAMES B. SWEENEY BY COMPLETELY RELIABLE WITNESSES.

| 0 | 5 | 10 | 15 | 20 | 25 | 30 | 35 | 40 | 45 | 50 |

PROBABLE LENGTH IN FEET

enough small fish in the lake to support a monster. Hubert Colchester, a professor at Ruskin College, Oxford University, disagrees with this belief. He says there are plenty of fish in the lake. Professor Taira Chikazawa, of Tokyo University, says he is convinced there is such an animal as the Loch Ness monster.

None of those disagreeing did so strongly. They seemed to be expressing little more than a weak doubt.

Here in the United States we appear to have more believers than nonbelievers. Of the many who have investigated the Loch Ness mystery, all are converts. After attending a meeting on the subject in the British Parliament, Dr. George R. Zug, of the Smithsonian Institution, said that he thought information showed there are large animals in Loch Ness. Professor A. W. Crompton, of Harvard University, said he found information on the Loch Ness monster "suggestive of a large aquatic animal." David B. Stone, Chairman of the New England Aquarium, found that photographs "support the belief that a large aquatic animal inhabits Loch Ness." A computer expert, Alan Gillespie, of the California Institute of Technology, said that his instruments indicated large animals in the lake.

The results of last year's Applied Science/New York Times Loch Ness expedition were published in *Technology Review*, a magazine put out by the Massachusetts Institute of Technology. There seems to be little or no disagreement over the fact that something large does live in the lake. The magazine pointed out one important finding: Certain areas of the lake showed more sightings than others; over half happened near river mouths and bays. This could have been due to any number of reasons. For instance, a sea monster would probably find that these locations offer cleaner water, better visibility, more fish upon which to feed, or fewer tourists to annoy them.

Food is important in the life of any animal, and the report states that "the loch contains an abundance of sea

trout, pike, stickleback, char, eels, and salmon." It estimated that Loch Ness holds up to 13 million adult salmon,
plus untold numbers of other fish. With this much food
available, as many as 156 large monsters could live in
Loch Ness.

There were other interesting points brought out by
the M.I.T. article. It pointed out that since electronic
equipment was used by the expedition, sonar played an
important part. This underwater device showed that
something large stirred up mud from the bottom. Unfortunately, a good deal of this mud settled on the eye of the
main underwater camera, and no pictures could then be
taken. One scientist stated that the silt was "stirred up
by the animal."

Three photographs taken by the expedition were
named as being important. Unfortunately, because of the
dark water, the silt, and Nessie's movements, the pictures
require a scientist to say what they show. To an average
person, they appear only as a blur. To someone trained in
the art of photo interpretation, they tell a story.

The first photograph was taken at 9:45 P.M. on June
19, 1976. It shows what appears to be a large pinkish
object.

The second photograph, taken at 10:30 P.M. on the
same day, shows a portion of a large cylindrical object.
This was only 10 feet from the camera.

The third photo was taken about 4:32 A.M. the
following day. It appears to be the upper portion of the
animal. The body surface is dappled.

Although Nessie has been a legend since A.D. 565, at
which time Saint Columba recorded his sighting, all
reports turned in before 1933 have been put aside. During
that year a road was built running along the western
shore of the lake. For the first time in history, trucks
were able to carry in modern sighting equipment. Since
then, scientific gear has become more accurate and more
plentiful. In 1933 radar and television had as yet not been

invented. Now both are in common use. Sonar and underwater listening devices also are on constant watch. These had never been heard of during the early thirties.

"All this gear helps us conclude one thing about Nessie," Lieutenant Commander S. T. E. Larter, R.N.R., said in the British publication *Mariner's Mirror*. "She, he, or it is in the lake. We must keep searching until we are able to identify what sort of monstrous beast lives in that body of water."